DEVOTIONS
TO MAKE YOU
smarter

OTHER BOOKS IN THE GROWING 2:52 LIBRARY

SMARTER • STRONGER • DEEPER • COOLER

DEVOTIONS
TO MAKE YOU
smarter

ED STRAUSS

ZONDER**kidz**

ZONDERVAN.com/
AUTHOR**TRACKER**
follow your favorite authors

Devotions to Make You Smarter
Copyright © 2007 by Edward Strauss

Requests for information should be addressed to:
Zonderkidz, *Grand Rapids, Michigan 49530*

Library of Congress Cataloging-in-Publication Data

Strauss, Ed, 1953-
    Devotions to make you smarter : by Ed Strauss.
        p. cm.
    ISBN-13: 0-310-71312-8 (softcover)
    ISBN-10: 0-310-71312-9 (softcover)
    1. Boys--Prayers and devotions--Juvenile literature. 2. Boys--Religious
life--Juvenile literature. 3. Boys--Conduct of life--Juvenile literature.
I. Title.
    BV4855.S76 2007
    242'.62--dc22

                                        2007022882

Editor: Barbara Scott
Art direction and design: Merit Alderink
Interior compositon: Christine Orejuela-Winkelman

Printed in the United States of America

09 10 11 12 13 14 /DCI/ 10 9 8 7 6 5 4 3

table of contents

devotion #1

TRACKING DOWN TREASURE

If you look for it as for silver and search
for it as for hidden treasure, then you
will ... find the knowledge of God.
For the LORD gives wisdom.
— Proverbs 2:4 – 6

King Solomon wrote this proverb, and he
knew all about searching for treasure. Once
a year his ships sailed south to a mysterious
African land called Ophir and came back
loaded down with gold. Solomon took in
more than twenty-five *tons* of gold a year! For
centuries, people have wondered where
those gold mines were, but the secret's
lost now.

What would you do if you found
a genuine treasure map that led to King

Solomon's mines or some other buried treasure? You'd be mighty interested in tracking down that treasure, right? Even if you had to crawl up mountains and hack through jungles, you'd keep at it. It's worth it for riches like that! Think how much you get into searching for treasure when it's just graphics in a computer game.

There's treasure in the Bible too — real treasure. The knowledge of God is worth more than buried treasure . . . and definitely more than computer-animated jewels. How does that figure? Simple. Having faith in Jesus guarantees you'll have eternal life in a fantastic paradise beyond your wildest dreams. Obeying God's Word gives you heavenly rewards that'll still glow like the sun a million years after diamonds have turned to dust.

Those are good reasons to read your Bible. Dig in, and you'll come out with your mind full of wisdom and your heart full of spiritual treasure.

devotion #2

USELESS INFORMATION

Moses was educated in all the wisdom of the Egyptians and was powerful in speech and action.

— Acts 7:22

Okay, so Moses had the best education Egypt could offer. He learned good stuff like math and hieroglyphics and how to build things. But he also had to memorize boring stuff like the names of every pharaoh who had ever lived, and study myths about pagan gods, and learn hymns to Khepri — the scarab-beetle, their creator-god. (When dung beetles hatched out of dung-balls, Egyptians thought they'd been miraculously created, so they worshiped the dung beetle as their creator.)

A lot of Egypt's wisdom wasn't very useful to Moses, and it may

sometimes seem the same to you in school today. You wonder why you need to memorize how many flies live in Australia. Or maybe you sit in class and study the elevation of the lowlands in South America or the formula for standard deviation. Sometimes you have to learn things that seem like a waste of good brain cells.

Don't zone out. A lot of subjects you might *think* are useless turn out to be very helpful after all — like boring math problems and science trivia about how flowers are pollinated. Relax. You have plenty of brain cells to spare.

It pays to pay attention and learn the boring subjects in school, even if they seem useless. You never know when they'll come in handy. Besides, you need to know them to pass.

devotion #3

DON'T LET THE BULL LOOSE!

'Do not do anything that endangers
your neighbor's life.'
— Leviticus 19:16

Now, *there's* a commonsense law that makes sense, huh? It's simple and to the point. But God didn't stop there. Most people really need things spelled out, so God spelled them out: If you have a mean bull that's got a bad habit of goring people with its horns, keep *el toro* locked up in a pen (Exodus 21:29). Do not let the bull loose, whatever you do! Some kids can't stand rules. They just wanna cut loose and go out and have fun. Yeah, but if you don't obey commonsense rules, you endanger other people's lives. You might leap off the diving board right on top of

another swimmer. Ignore the maximum-number-of-kids-on-a-trampoline rule, and you'll bounce some kid off the trampoline onto his head. Every summer, lots of kids are rushed from pools and trampolines to the hospital. Rules are there for a reason.

You may wonder why God put so many laws in the Bible — especially in the Old Testament. He did it because he loves people and doesn't want to see them hurt. That's why he wrote laws to protect people's property — so someone couldn't just come along and take what didn't belong to them. That's why he wrote laws against stealing and lying and cheating others. That's why he made laws about being kind to other people.

You're smart to obey God's laws. It's great if you understand why the rules exist. But even if you don't understand, remember, God put rules there to protect you and others.

Devotion #4
LAY THAT CLICKER DOWN

If you give the scroll to someone who cannot read, and say, "Read this, please," he will answer, "I don't know how to read."

— Isaiah 29:12

For hundreds of years, goat herders in Egypt kept finding ancient scrolls in the desert sands. Since they couldn't read, they didn't have a clue that these scrolls were worth hundreds of thousands of dollars — even millions of dollars — and the goat herders burned them to heat water for tea. Oh, man! Talk about expensive cups of tea!

You may think that was crazy, but lots of boys today are in similar shape. No, they're not burning ancient scrolls, but they can barely read. It's a

good thing jugs of poison have skulls and crossbones on their labels, 'cause some guys can't read poison warnings. Now, it's one thing if a kid has a learning disability — you can sympathize with his having a hard time — but there's no excuse for sheer, plain, flopped-on-the-couch-with-cookies-and-a-clicker laziness.

If you don't read well, what can you do about it? Simple. Read more. Exercise your brain. If you really wanted to get on a swim team and weren't making it, what would you do? You'd start swimming like crazy, right? And you *would* get better. It's the same with reading. Don't read well? Read more. Don't understand some word? Ask what it means.

Unhook your fingers from the clicker, tumble off the couch, crawl away from the TV, and go find a good book. If you're *really* desperate, read the back of a cereal box. Better yet, read your Bible.

devotion #5
SHOUTING MATCH MISTAKE

But the men of Judah responded even more harshly than the men of Israel ... So all the men of Israel deserted David.

— 2 Samuel 19:43; 20:2

In this story, enemies had chased King David across the Jordan River. When danger was past, the men of Judah brought David back. Then the Israelites showed up, all steamed because no one had called them to help bring the king across the river. They argued until they got in a shouting match. In the end, the boys from Judah may have won the shouting match, but it got the men of Israel so upset that they rebelled against David's kingdom.

These days, instead of arguing over who gets to have a boat ride with

the king, kids fight over whose turn it is to manage the TV clicker or who gets what seat in the car. The arguing gets louder until someone wins the shouting match. Some victory. Then Mom or Dad takes away everyone's TV privileges or cancels the outing and no one rides in the car.

There are smart ways to avoid shouting matches. The men of Judah could've said, "Oh, man! We forgot to invite you? Sorry. Our bad!" It's often ridiculously easy to make peace. You may not want to let someone take his turn first or sit in a certain seat, but think about it — is it really worth it to keep arguing until everyone suffers?

Sure, everyone wants to insist on his or her rights. Everyone wants a fair turn. But it's not worth losing a friend over or getting everyone grounded.

devotion #6
DO THE MATH

"Suppose one of you wants to build a tower.
Will he not first sit down and estimate
the cost to see if he has enough
money to complete it?"

— Luke 14:28

One day Jesus was talking about being a
disciple. He compared it to building a tower.
He explained how important it was to think
things through before rushing into action.
Otherwise, you'll spend all your money
building the basement and then have
no cash left to build the tower itself.
Bummer. Not only are you out all that
cash, but you still don't have a tower.
Worse yet, everyone who sees your
half-built building will mock you.

You can apply Jesus' advice to any project you're excited about. Think about what it'll cost you before you actually start! Like, if you want a tree fort but you can only afford three boards, don't just run out, buy the boards, and nail 'em up — 'cause for the next year kids will stare up at those three pitiful boards and joke, "Niiiice tree fort, Tarzan!"

Sit down and take some time to estimate the cost; then count your cash and find out what you can scrounge. While you're at it, ask your parents for advice. You might be surprised, but grown-ups are good at that kind of stuff. They have to estimate the costs on zillions of things. So run your plans past Mom or Dad. They'll give you a good reality check.

When you get an idea for a project, it's fine to get excited. *Still.* Pull out a piece of paper, grab a calculator, and do the math. Know what you're getting into.

devotion #7
ANGELS FREEZING TONGUES

"How will this be?"

Mary asked the angel.

— Luke 1:34

When the angel Gabriel told Mary she'd have a baby, she asked, "How will this be?" So Gabriel explained. But when Gabriel told Zechariah that his wife would have a baby and Zech asked, "How can I be sure of this?" (Luke 1:18), the angel struck him dumb! For nine months! Are angels tougher on boys than girls? No. It was all in their attitudes. See, Mary believed; she just had a question. Zech didn't believe.

If you don't understand something in the Bible, it's okay to ask questions. If you wonder how God parted the Red Sea, ask your parents. They may tell you that God performed a miracle. Maybe

you already knew that, but you wanted to know the mechanics of it. So ask someone else. Check it out with your youth group leader or read a Bible question-and-answer book. They may be able to tell you that the sea spread apart because "all that night the Lᴏʀᴅ drove the sea back with a strong east wind" (Exodus 14:21). Whoa! That was some wind!

There are commonsense answers to most Bible questions. Sure, sometimes God's power will be way beyond our understanding. Why not? He's God. He invented matter and energy, and he can make them do some mind-bending stuff. Just about all we can say is, "It's a miracle." But you can *ask*. God won't strike you with lightning, and the angel Gabriel won't freeze your tongue.

devotion #8
SMART STRATEGIES, SMART MOVES

Joshua marched up from Gilgal with his
entire army ... After an all-night march from
Gilgal, Joshua took them by surprise.

—Joshua 10:7, 9

The city of Gibeon was an ally of Israel, so
when five armies surrounded Gibeon, Joshua got
his one army together and set out to help. If they
marched by day, lots of Canaanites would see 'em
and run ahead to warn the enemy. So what's
Joshua do? He marches his army eighteen
miles from Gilgal to Gibeon *at night*. The
next morning as the enemy troops are
crawling out of bed, the Israelites attack!
God then performed miracles and helped
the Israelites win the battle!

It pays to use your brain and not
just your muscles. If you're trying to put

the chain back on your bike, it doesn't help to try to force it on and get all sweaty and frustrated. You'll just cut your knuckles. Or if you're playing checkers, there's no way you'll win by just moving your men forward as fast as you can. And in computer games — even if your character has lots of lives — you can't just charge in and take hit after hit.

You need to think and plan. In any game or sport, it helps big-time to have speed and strength on your side, but it's often strategy — smart moves — that determines who wins and who loses. Strategy is important in war, in football, in chess, and in computer games. In fact, thinking things out before you make your move is important in *all* areas of life.

Got a problem? Don't try to solve it with brute strength alone. You aren't King Kong. Use your brain! And pray for God's help. He's smarter and stronger than anyone!

Devotion #9
BEEFING UP YOUR BRAIN POWER

To these four young men God gave knowledge and understanding of all kinds of literature and learning.

— Daniel 1:17

King Nebuchadnezzar wanted some new servants, so he told his man Ashpenaz to pick youth who were good at learning and quick to understand. Ashpenaz tapped Daniel and his friends, gave them a crash course in Babylonian, plopped big stacks of literature in front of them, and said, "Here, learn this." Sure, Daniel and pals were smart, but they were overwhelmed. So they prayed, and God helped their brains learn even better than they normally did.

Maybe you're naturally smart: your dad's a rocket scientist and your mom's a nuclear physicist, so of course you were born with a beefed-up brain. But what happens when you need to learn stuff that's way over your head? Sure, you can study extra, but even smart kids burn out. And hey, let's be real: chances are good that your parents aren't rocket scientists or nuclear physicists, and you're about average in the brains department. What then?

Do what you can do: pay attention in class and study hard. Those things are huge. But if you don't want your brain to wear out like an overused eraser, pray for extra ability to understand. Need wisdom and knowledge? James 1:5 says, "If any of you lacks wisdom, he should ask God, who gives generously to all." That's a promise! But you gotta ask.

Remember, God's not limited to helping you with just the stuff you're naturally good at. God helped Daniel and his friends with "all kinds of learning."

devotion #10
LOSING STUFF ALL THE TIME

These searched for their family records,
but they could not find them and so were
excluded from the priesthood.

— Ezra 2:62

In Israel, only those in the tribe of Levi could
be priests. It wasn't enough to say you were
a Levite, either—you had to prove it. That's
why Levites kept family records to show they
were descended from Levi. But three guys—
Hobaiah, Hakkoz, and Barzillai—got careless.
When it came time to show their records, Hob,
Hak, and Barz tore their houses apart to find
them—but they couldn't. Too bad, boys.
You can't be priests. Got a plan B?
Being disorganized and careless
can cost you big-time. If your teacher

hands you a permission slip but you forget to give
it to your mom, well, she can't sign something she's
never seen. You just missed a fun outing. Forget your
homework, and it costs you marks. Lose your friend's
phone number, and you skip that sleepover. Misplace a
rented video game, and you pay so many late charges
you could've *bought* the game four times over.

If you have a habit of forgetting stuff or
misplacing important papers, then start new habits
today. First, make sure you always put your homework
in your school bag. Second, give your mom or dad
notices or permission slips as soon as you get home.
Third, don't leave video games or other important stuff
lying just anywhere. *Always* put them where you can
find them again.

If you don't want to be scrambling around
searching and crying like Hob, Hak, and Barz, do
yourself a favor and get organized.

Devotion #11
WORKING OUT THE DETAILS

The ark is to be 450 feet long, 75 feet wide and 45 feet high ... Put a door in the side of the ark and make lower, middle and upper decks.

— Genesis 6:15 – 16

God gave Noah the basic measurements for the ark, and then Noah spent many years building it. Obviously Noah had to figure out quite a few details. He had to think how to reinforce the beams so the ship wouldn't break up in the storm. He had to invent systems to feed the animals and pipe water to them. He had to dream up a way to suck fresh air into the ark so they didn't all suffocate.

It's the same today: you often know what God wants you to do, but

you have to figure out the details. For example, you know you're supposed to go to school. But you don't pass the grade by simply sitting at your desk. You have to plug your brain in and figure stuff out. You may wonder, "Can't God just give me the answers to the test?" You wish!

That's where your brain has to kick in. You have to study and really wrap your mind around problems. Sometimes they're so complicated you think you're mud-wrestling alligators. You're trying hard but not getting it. Well, keep at it and you'll succeed. Pray for God to help your brain work well — then *use* the thing.

God spells out goals and guidelines just as he did for Noah — and he'll even help you with the details — but you have to do your part and think.

Devotion #12
CHECKING YOUR MOTIVES

The LORD searches every heart and understands every motive behind the thoughts.

— 1 Chronicles 28:9

God hears every word you speak. He knows every thought you think. And get this: he knows the motives behind every thought you think. God shines a light into your heart, checking out what motivates you, what makes you do what you do. You ain't hiding nothin' from him! No wonder King David said, "Before a word is on my tongue you know it completely" (Psalm 139:4). You bet God does! He knew what you were gonna say before you even thought it.

At the end of your life when you stand before the judgment seat of Christ, you'll be rewarded for all the

good you've done, and all the garbage will be burned away. At that time, you'll be asked to give account to God for every thoughtless word you've said. Jesus said that if you even think of doing sin, sometimes it's as if you've already done the deed.

What effect does this have on you to know that God knows the motives behind your actions? Don't let it worry you. Sure, you should have a healthy respect for God, but more than anything, double-check your motives. And ask God to forgive you when you slip up. He loves you, and he's on your side!

God knows absolutely everything you do, say, think, or *think* about thinking. That's a good reason to do good, speak good, and even think good.

Devotion #13
DULL AXES, DULL MINDS

If the ax is dull and its edge unsharpened,
more strength is needed but skill
will bring success.

— Ecclesiastes 10:10

Back in King Solomon's day, some
woodcutters couldn't be bothered to stop
chopping long enough to go to the blacksmith
to get their axes sharpened. They kept hacking
away with a dull blade, and the job kept getting
harder . . . and harder . . . and harder. Finally,
they were using all their strength and sweating
like pigs just to make a dent in the tree.
C'mon, guys! It doesn't take Sherlock
Holmes to figure this mystery out.
You think those woodcutters
were clueless? What about the kid

who gets a complex toy, doesn't bother to read the instructions, and starts trying to assemble the parts? Not exactly brilliant. Sure, with enough glue you can make just about anything stick together, but would you really want that hideous thing in your room? Or what about the kid who won't take time to tighten a loose wheel on his skateboard? Good way to save time? Not.

Save yourself a headache by reading instructions. Study how things are supposed to fit rather than grunting and groaning and forcing parts together. Things will fit together, work well, and look cool if you take the time to do it right. And you spare yourself a cracked skull by taking the time to tighten loose skateboard wheels and adjust the brakes on your bike.

Don't go through life like a dull woodcutter with a dull ax. Sure, muscles are great and glue is awesome, but using a little skill and wisdom makes things work easier and better.

Devotion #14
A WISE MAN'S ATTITUDE

Do not rebuke a mocker or he will hate you; rebuke a wise man and he will love you.

— Proverbs 9:8

Why, when you think of a certain kid, would you describe him as a *mocker*? Well, these days you probably wouldn't. Instead, you'd say, "Man, does that kid have a mouth on him!" Or, "What a know-it-all!" Back in Bible days they had a simple name for a kid like that — *mocker*. No matter what you tried to tell this kid, he'd mock you.

Try to set him straight on something, and he just hates you. Why should he listen? He knows it all already. Of course he *doesn't*, but he's

so defensive and proud that he can't bear to listen to any kind of correction. So he tries to act smart and uses sarcastic humor to attack anyone who tries to straighten him out. You learn quickly not to try to tell him anything.

A know-it-all is a pain to be around. So be wise. When your friends try to teach you how not to goof up, or your parents rebuke you after you've blown it, listen to what they say and learn from it. It'll keep you from making the same mistake again. When someone goes to the trouble to correct you, it shows they care about you.

Don't get into it with a mocker, and don't be a mocker yourself. You'll learn a lot more and be a lot easier to live with if you're willing to listen to correction.

Devotion #15
HOWLING KILLER MICE

Ask the animals, and they will teach you, or the birds of the air, and they will tell you; or speak to the earth, and it will teach you, or let the fish of the sea inform you.

—Job 12:7–8

The Bible isn't saying to go snorkeling and start quizzing schools of fish. It's not saying you should go to the zoo and ask the elephants to help you with your history assignment. (Their memory isn't that good.) This verse is saying that if you watch animals in action, you can learn a lot about God. Like Proverbs 6:6 says: "Go to the ant ... consider its ways and be wise!"

Nature shows are good for learning about the hand of God on earth. You learn that elephants travel hundreds of miles through jungles to find a single salt lick or that a South American bird goes wild doing a high-speed moonwalk to attract females. And what about the grasshopper mouse that hunts deadly scorpions and howls like a little wolf? Talk about wild! It seems God really cut loose when creating certain critters.

When you tune in to the animals, you learn cool stuff about nature and see the amazing thought that went into creating creatures. You begin to get an idea of how superintelligent God is. After all, he's the one who designed every creature — from the microscopic to the big — with cool features, like birds with built-in navigation systems. And how about those *killer mice* . . .

The more you study nature, the more wise you become as you learn to appreciate God's wisdom and design in creation.

Devotion #16
ADMITTING YOU DON'T KNOW

"Do you understand what you are reading?" Philip asked. "How can I," he said, "unless someone explains it to me?"

— Acts 8:30 – 31

A Christian named Philip was walking down the road when he saw an Ethiopian official riding by in a chariot. The guy was reading Isaiah chapter 53. Now, Philip knew this chapter was a prophecy about Jesus, so he asked the Ethiopian if he understood it. When the man admitted that he didn't, Philip hopped up in the chariot with him and began to teach him about Jesus.

Ever been sitting in class when the teacher's trolling up and down the aisles, looking over everyone's shoulder

at their work? The teacher sees you scrunching up your face and asks, "Do you need help?" What do you say? Or, ever been playing a video game and Gazooka the Ogre is stomping you? Then your kid sister skips up and says, "I can tell you how to beat him." What do you do?

Okay, okay, if you want to let Gazooka continue stomping you until all your lives are gone rather than let your kid sister be able to say she saved you, that's one thing. But when you really need help — like with interpreting the words of the Bible, your schoolwork, or some serious problem — that's not the time to play cool and say no. If you need help, ask for it. Who else you gonna ask? Your dog? He doesn't know.

Don't be too proud to admit that you don't understand something. Asking questions is how you get answers.

Devotion #17

MEMOS AND REMINDERS

You will have these tassels to look at and so you will remember all the commands of the LORD.

— Numbers 15:39

God commanded the Jews to wear tassels — little twisty tails of cloth that dangled on the bottom of their robes. Every time someone walked by, you saw the tassels swinging on the edge of their robes, and they saw the tassels dangling on your robes. And everyone was reminded, "Oh, yeah! We're God's people, and we're supposed to obey God's commands."

Seem weird? Well, having strange, out-of-the-ordinary reminders helps! People are forgetful, and kids with exciting things on their minds are *especially*

forgetful. Has your mom ever sent you to do something and you got tripped up on the way and never arrived? Ever forget to throw your clothes in the laundry or clean the cat's litter box? We forget little stuff all the time, and it's also easy to forget the *big* things that God wants us to do — like treating others with kindness.

It's no longer the fashion for boys to wear robes with cutesy-tootsy tassels. Bet you're glad for *that*, huh? These days people wear T-shirts that talk about Jesus or put God posters on their bedroom walls. Some people scribble memos on their hand or even tie strings around their finger to help them remember. Some people's fridges are so full of magnets holding messages, their entire fridge has become magnetized. (Just kidding.)

We do lots of things today to remind ourselves of important stuff. Do whatever it takes to remember God's Word.

devotion #18
REALLY LEARNING

... Always learning but never able to acknowledge the truth.

— 2 Timothy 3:7

Back in Paul's day, some people were like Curious George — constantly interested in new stuff without thinking about the big picture. They gathered knowledge nonstop, but all their scattered education did was fill up their minds with scraps of information. They still didn't acknowledge the truth, meaning they knew all *about* the truth, but they hadn't let it change their lives. They were like squirrels storing away nuts they never ate.

It's the same today with some kids raised in Christian homes: they know all about the Bible and Jesus

dying on the cross, but they've never given their heart to him. Other kids have taken that step — and that's a terrific start — but then slacked off on living as a Christian. They learn about the Bible, but it seems like just a collection of interesting stories about talking donkeys and battles and Noah building an ark and yada yada.

It's great to learn more about the Bible, but the most important thing is to know Jesus and to live your life so that it really counts! Don't just read the Bible, but accept it and let it change your life. When you actually acknowledge the truth, it hits you between the eyes: the Bible's about a life-changing relationship with God. The interesting stories are just pepperoni on the pizza.

It's cool to learn about all the bits and pieces, but don't miss the big picture. Get an actual knowledge of the truth, and then keep learning!

Devotion #19
PERFECT MESSAGE, IMPERFECT DELIVERY

Blessed is the one who reads the words of this prophecy, and blessed are those who hear it and take to heart what is written in it.

— Revelation 1:3

The apostle John was a Jew who spoke great Aramaic (*air-ah-may-ik*), but his Greek was kind of rough. Some scribes probably helped him write the Gospel of John, so the Greek came out perfectly. But when he wrote the book of Revelation, John was alone. Bible scholars say that John's Greek was so rough in places, it's clear that Greek wasn't his first language. So what? Revelation has a powerful, encouraging message. It has tons of stuff you need to know.

It's the same when your parents are talking to you: listen to the message.

When your mom asks why you haven't cleaned your bedroom yet, try to understand what she means. True, maybe you *did* pick the clothes up off the floor, but she's looking at the unmade bed and the messy desk.

You may feel that she's not quite right. You *did* clean up . . . sort of. But accept your parents' message even if the delivery isn't perfect. Sure, they may mix up some details or forget some stuff, but is what they're saying right or not? And if it is, then take it to heart instead of picking it apart.

You're blessed if you read Revelation and blessed if you take it to heart — even if John's Greek wasn't perfect. You're also blessed if you listen to your parents and take what they say to heart.

devotion #20

BUILT UP, NOT PUFFED UP

knowledge puffs up, but love builds up.

— *1 Corinthians 8:1*

If you just get knowledge but don't have love, you end up with a big head that is empty of true meaning. You get puffed up. It's like a bullfrog puffing up to try to look bigger. Is he really bigger? Nah. He's just full of hot air. And since he can't hold his breath forever, the ugly green dwarf will soon go back down to his real size.

"Knowledge puffs up." You can fill your head with facts and figures, but if you don't have love, you won't know how to *use* that information properly. It's just taking up space. You might as well be stuffing your skull full of sawdust. You'll be like the scarecrow in *The Wizard of Oz* who was so completely clueless that he set off walking down the road to find a brain.

"Love builds up." The most important things in life are to love God and to love your neighbor as yourself. If you love yourself, you'll take care of yourself and build yourself up — like a bodybuilder building up muscles. If you love others, you'll say kind things that will encourage them. Instead of showing off how smart you are or quoting facts to cut others down, build them up. (So let's not make fun of the scarecrow of Oz. He actually *had* a brain all along.)

If you have love, then you build yourself up and you build others up. Avoid the bullfrog syndrome. Live a built-up life, not a puffed-up life.

devotion #21
LEARNING FROM THE MASTER TEACHER

When they saw the courage of Peter
and John and realized that they
were unschooled, ordinary men, they were
astonished and they took note that these
men had been with Jesus.

— Acts 4:13

Peter and John were telling the
crowds about Jesus when the temple
guards snagged them and dragged them
before the top religious council. Now,
the religious rulers could see that Peter
and John were just regular guys. They
were rough-and-tumble working-class
guys and hadn't received higher education, yet these boys were so sure

of the facts and so bold declaring them, it was clear they'd been with *the* master teacher, Jesus.

Now, like Peter and John, you are probably a regular guy — you try to do your best, and there is something you are really good at. Maybe you aren't pulling an A+ in math, but you love to read. Maybe you're good at designing and creating art. Maybe you are very generous with your friends. Maybe there is something that makes you stand out in a crowd. Most likely, you have your strengths and your weaknesses, and you blend in with average people.

If you know Jesus and you know the Bible, you're not just one more average person. If you know the Man, then you know the truly important things about life, and you can't help but stand out. Get close to Jesus and it will show! Other people can't help but notice something different about you.

It's important to be smart about science and math and other stuff, but it's most important of all to have a relationship with Jesus.

Devotion #22
IMAGINATION — GOOD AND BAD

The LORD saw . . . that every inclination of the thoughts of his heart was only evil all the time.

— Genesis 6:5

Before the flood — a few hundred years before Noah was born — there was an amazing Age of Invention. Unfortunately, it was mostly evil Cain's kids doing the inventing. A guy named Jabal started making tents and herding cattle; Jubal invented all kinds of musical instruments; and Tubal-Cain was the granddaddy of all metalworkers (Genesis 4:20 – 22). You'd think all this new stuff was great, but they had no use for God, and by Noah's day, men's imaginations were evil all the time.

In modern times, knowledge is increasing so fast that you can't keep up with all the new information. And talk about inventions! In your grandparents' day, TVs had just been invented, and computers were huge clunkers that took up whole rooms. And video games? They didn't even exist when your mom and dad were kids. These days, computer games with powerful graphics and more RAM than a mountain sheep fit in the palm of your hand.

But does all the amazing technology we have solve the world's problems? No. Despite a lot of cool inventions, people are as selfish as ever. Knowledge alone doesn't change people's hearts. Some great Christian inventors and scientists are using their imagination to help make the world a better place. Unfortunately, some scientists dream up some truly ungodly things.

It's cool to have a fantastic imagination — God gave it to you. Just be sure you also seek God and use that imagination to dream up good things.

Devotion #23

MAGIC BOOKS DISAPPEAR!

A number who had practiced sorcery brought their scrolls together and burned them publicly.

— Acts 19:19

The apostle Paul spent a couple years in Ephesus. This city was a center for witches and sorcerers and magicians. Then lots of these guys became Christians and decided to burn their "spell" books. They torched 50,000 drachmas' worth! Since a drachma is worth about a day's wages, that's a lot of abracadabras going up in smoke! (*Poof!* Watch me make these magic books disappear!) These guys were serious about cleaning the junk out of their lives.

Today there are tons of spell books and movies around. We're not talking

about Merlin in the movie *Sword in the Stone* or other fantasy stories about magic. We're talking about the old pagan religion of witchcraft itself. People read the witchy books because they're interested in secret wisdom and figure these books have it. *Not smart.* Or they figure that by mumbling magical rhymes they'll get quick answers to problems. *Not.* It's just bad poetry.

If you really want wisdom, plug into the one true God — not the false goat-god of witchcraft. Our God has the answers. He also has the power to give genuine answers to prayer. His miracles may take a while to happen, but they're worth waiting for. Best of all, faith in Jesus gives you eternal life in heaven, something witchcraft can never do.

Take a tip from the ancient sorcerers of Ephesus! When they found new life in Jesus, they gladly burned all their old spell books! They didn't care how much it cost them.

Devotion #24
FIGHTING AND BITING

The Lord's servant must not quarrel;
instead, he must be kind to everyone.

— 2 Timothy 2:24

Who is this servant of the Lord who must not quarrel? Does this verse mean that pastors and missionaries shouldn't argue, but it's okay for everybody else to bite one another's heads off? No. The Bible warns, "If you keep on biting and devouring each other, watch out or you will be destroyed by each other" (Galatians 5:15). God doesn't want us to be spiritual cannibals! We're all God's servants and shouldn't quarrel over silly stuff.

You may think, "Okay, I can stop quarreling, but do I have to be kind to everyone — even to my sister?" Well,

if you just stop quarreling without being kind, you'll be right back at it at the drop of a hat (as soon as the adults leave the room). But if you're considerate and kind, then you'll stop arguing and stay stopped. You may say, "Hey, my sister really bugs me." *Still*.

This thing about being kind to others goes back to what Jesus said about loving everyone, even your enemies. Jesus said to be considerate to others just like you'd want them to be considerate to you. It's hard to bite your tongue when other kids start arguments over dumb things, but the point is, you don't have to get into it. Some things are worth arguing over, but most things aren't. Know the difference.

If you want to follow Jesus and be God's servant instead of a spiritual cannibal, there are a few ground rules. One, be kind to everyone. Two, don't quarrel over piddly stuff.

Devotion #25
LOST: ONE HUNDRED WISE MEN

Where is the wise man? Where is the scholar? Where is the philosopher of this age? Has not God made foolish the wisdom of the world?

— 1 Corinthians 1:20

It's good to be a wise man who figures stuff out and can say exactly the right thing so that a thousand people leap to their feet clapping. It's cool to be a scholar who digs into the Bible and discovers all kinds of ancient facts. It's great if you're a philosopher lost deep in thought, figuring out the mysteries of the universe. But as smart as all these people are, they can miss out on basic stuff. We're not talking about your dad not being able to figure out how to set the microwave timer or some kid who

can win at a high-speed computer game but can't remember where he put his homework. We're talking about brilliant dudes who are clueless about the ABC's of Christian life itself.

A lot of supersmart people can't get their minds around the simple truths of the Bible. Sure, they may know how to map DNA and write computer programs and other complicated stuff, but they're clueless when it comes to understanding that Jesus died for their sins or that it's important to love others. If you don't live the basic Bible stuff, being wise about everything else is just icing without a cake.

So study and learn as much as you can. You should go whole hog for education. Just make sure you understand the simple, important truths of the Bible.

devotion #26
CONTROLLING YOUR THOUGHTS

We take captive every thought to make it obedient to Christ.

— 2 Corinthians 10:5

Jesus said that you should not only worship God with all your heart, but that you should worship him with your whole mind (Matthew 22:37). But how can you do that if your mind's running all over the place? You have to gather your thoughts. You have to capture them and make them obedient to Christ. The Greek word for *captive* in this verse means "to take prisoner." Picture prisoners marching along in chains and someone's poking them, saying, "Okaaay, boys, keep moving."

Would you say your thoughts are under control? Or is your brain more like a zoo where every single monkey

has broken out of its cage and is swinging all over the place, screaming and going bananas? Example: if you're a Christian, you know you're supposed to forgive others. But if someone crosses you, does your mind plan a hundred ways to hang him up by his toes?

No matter how wild an imagination you were born with, you don't need to let it take you on a mental roller-coaster ride. Maybe you're spacey or creative, but that's not a reason to give your mind an all-day pass to the amusement park. You can control your thoughts, but you have to be militant about it. You have to be aggressive.

You don't want to end up brain-dead from all the confusion, so forget the saying "Take no prisoners." Take your thoughts prisoner. Take as many prisoners as you can. Then put those captive thoughts to work for Jesus.

Devotion #27
WRONG PLANET? SOOO SORRY!

*Let your astrologers come forward,
those stargazers who make predictions month
by month, let them save you from what is
coming ... They cannot even save themselves.*

— Isaiah 47:13 – 14

Astrologers believe that distant stars
and planets cause things to happen here on
earth. They divide the stars into twelve
zones, and if you were born when the sun
was in the Gemini zone, they say your
"sign" is Gemini and the planet Mercury
rules you. And if the planet Venus was
in the Pisces zone then, well, dude,
you're gonna be *soooo* romantic.

Astrologers make predictions
like, "Attention all Libras! July is a

great month for summer vacations." Or they make day-by-day predictions: "October 22 is a good day for money and friendship. Start a business while cooking barbecue." Is that what you want to put your faith in? C'mon! How scientific is that? Studying the stars lets you know when to break your piggy bank and run to the corner store? Really?

There are twelve "signs," and each sign needs a planet. But for thousands of years people could see only five planets, so they said that some planets ruled two signs. Then astronomers discovered Pluto in 1930. Oh, boy! Up till then, astrologers claimed that Mars ruled the signs Aries and Scorpio. Pluto had been there all along, but suddenly in 1930 it gets the job. "So sorry, Scorpios! Our bad! You can't stay on Mars! We're shipping you to Pluto!" And now we know that Pluto isn't a planet after all. What a joke!

God's Word warns against putting your trust in things other than God to save you. If you want wisdom on how to live your life, you'll get real smarts by reading your Bible.

Devotion #28
QUALITY RESEARCH

Since I myself have carefully investigated everything from the beginning, it seemed good also to me to write an orderly account.

— Luke 1:3

Luke was a physician living in Greece. It had been almost thirty years since Jesus had been crucified and raised from the dead, and Luke wanted to write a gospel for Greek Christians. He didn't want to do a sloppy job, either. He wanted to see the places where things had happened and interview eyewitnesses. So Luke sailed all the way to Israel to investigate the facts. He then wrote an orderly account, meaning an organized, easy-to-understand, and reliable report.

What about you? When your teacher tells you to write a report on

something, do you check things out on the ground, investigate on the Internet, and interview people who know about it? Do you check your facts carefully, or do you slide by with as little work as possible — just enough to pass? Or if your mom wants to know who's responsible for making a mess, do you check the facts carefully before blaming someone? Do people know they can trust you as a source of reliable information?

The kind of careful research Luke did stands the test of time. You can be sure that your faith is built upon the truth because Luke double-checked and triple-checked his information. So take care with your research. Make sure it's not only accurate, but that people can easily understand it. This is true for schoolwork as well as telling others the facts about Jesus.

When it comes to investigating facts and explaining them simply, Luke stands out as a top researcher and an example to follow.

Devotion #29
BITING YOUR TONGUE

He who holds his tongue is wise ... Even a fool is thought wise if he keeps silent.
— Proverbs 10:19; 17:28

There are times — lots of times, in fact — when it's wise to hold your tongue. That doesn't mean grabbing your tongue with your hands — you can hold that sucker just fine with your teeth. Teeth are practically made for the job. That's not hard for a wise person. But for a fool, trying to hang on to his tongue is like trying to stay on a rodeo bull.

Some kids never stop talking. Know anyone like that? It's fine to be a talker. Chatty people are fun to be around, but not if their mouth pours out a nonending stream of foolish jokes and grossness. Some kids talk about things they shouldn't just to see how many laughs

they can get — like if their little brother wet his bed and they tell all his friends.

It's fun to joke around, but you gotta know what to joke about and when to zip your lip. If you know how to do that, you're wise. In fact, considering how fools like to talk, people may even think a fool is wise if he keeps silent. Like, maybe his mouth was full of pizza and he couldn't talk, but at least he missed saying something stupid.

Know when to hold on to your tongue. It doesn't take a lot of brains to keep your mouth shut, but you gotta use the brains you have. Keep pizza handy if you have to.

Devotion #30
ACTUALLY ASKING QUESTIONS

They spoke against God, saying, "Can God
spread a table in the desert? When he
struck the rock, water gushed out . . .
But can he also give us food?"
— Psalm 78:19 – 20

The Israelites had been dying of thirst
in the desert, so Moses grabbed his staff,
whacked a rock, and voilà — instant water
fountain! "Okay," the Israelites said. "So
God can do miracles to give us water.
Big deal! But can he *also* give us food?"
The answer was plain: of *course* he
could! But the Israelites were showing
that they didn't really trust God.
Here's a modern example of an
insincere question: "How come all I do

is homework, and I never get to do anything fun?" Or this one: "How come I only got to go to the waterslides and I can't go to the movies afterward?" Usually the complainer already knows the answer, but his brain's gone into lockdown and he's just not getting it.

There are good answers to sincere questions, but honestly, how do you expect God or your parents or anybody to respond to a child who simply won't stop complaining or repeating a request? The sad thing about complaints is that they show the person isn't thankful for all the good already received.

It's fine to ask questions, but make sure you're actually asking questions, not just complaining. There's a big difference.

Devotion #31
LEARNING THE GUR AND BÙR

Terah took his son Abram . . . and together they set out from Ur of the Chaldeans.

— Genesis 11:31

Abram lived around four thousand years ago and herded sheep for a living, but he wasn't uneducated. In Ur where he grew up, boys went to school and learned to read and write and do math. Like, they had to calculate how many gur of grain grew on 4,325 bùr of land. (Hint: One bùr is about 6.3 hectares and produces 30 gur — 9,000 liters — of barley.) Got that? No? Well, Abram had to learn it.

Do you find math hard? Might as well get used to it. Kids no longer have to know the gur and bùr of Ur, but there are still lots of multiplication and division and fractions and decimals to

learn. You might ask, "Why should I study math? What good will it do me?" That's like asking, "Why do I need to study the Bible? How will it help me?"

You need to understand math so you can calculate how much money to save or how to count your change at the store. You need to know math when measuring boards for a tree fort. You need math for oodles of everyday stuff. It's the same with reading your Bible. Like math, it may sometimes seem theoretical and dry, but learning how God wants you to live and how to treat others is very practical.

Ever since Abram was a boy in ancient Ur, kids have been learning both math and the Bible. We can't live without either one.

devotion #32
WISE ABOUT BASIC STUFF

From infancy you have known the holy
Scriptures, which are able to make you
wise for salvation.

— 2 Timothy 3:15

A Bible guy named Timothy had a Jewish mom and a Greek dad. Down in Israel, Jews wrote Bible verses on their doors or on pieces of paper that they folded and stuffed inside tiny boxes tied to their hands and foreheads. Tim's mom probably didn't make these kinds of decor and fashion statements — her Greek husband wasn't into that — but she did teach Tim the Bible.

If you've grown up in a Christian home, then your parents have probably told you Bible stories since you were

old enough to hang on to the furniture and walk. As you got older, they quoted Bible verses to let you know how to behave. For example, if you know you're supposed to consider other people's needs, then no kids will go hungry 'cause you oinked down all the pie. Simple stuff, but it helped make you wise.

Best of all, when you listen to the Bible you find out that God loved you so much that he sent Jesus to die on the cross to save you. You might say, "Wise? That's wisdom? That's really basic stuff." Yes, it is. It's wise if you take it to heart, but it's very foolish if you ignore it.

You may not always be thrilled to hear Bible rules, but if you take them in like Timothy did, they'll not only give you faith but teach you how to live.

Devotion #33
DEMOLITION DERBY

We demolish arguments and every pretension that sets itself up against the knowledge of God.

—2 Corinthians 10:5

Some smart people have a dumb problem: they don't want to obey God. So they come up with all kinds of *pretensions* why God doesn't exist. (A pretension is a claim or an argument—in this case, a *pretend* argument.) Or if they don't want to live a godly life, they claim that the Bible isn't true or that its rules don't apply today. If they can convince themselves that there's no God and that the Bible's outdated, they can live as they please.

As a Christian, you have the power to demolish these anti-God

arguments. Picture a big bulldozer with a wide blade demolishing a flimsy house. This doesn't mean you should drive up in an actual bulldozer or use pushy arguments like, "You're dumb if you don't believe the Bible!" It doesn't mean intimidating people by using big words they don't understand, and it doesn't mean arguing angrily.

The things you use to demolish false claims are *spiritual* weapons like prayer and God's wisdom. Of course, God also expects you to study the questions and come up with intelligent answers. You might hear someone say, "Jesus was a great teacher, but aren't there many ways to God?" You gotta know enough about it to answer, "No, Jesus claimed that he was God's Son, and that he was the only way to God."

You have the power of God and the wisdom of his Word on your side. Now get ready to do some demolition!

devotion #34
PLANNING, PLOTTING, AND PRAYING

Many are the plans in a man's heart, but it is the LORD's purpose that prevails.

— Proverbs 19:21

If we didn't need brains and didn't need to plan stuff, God could've filled our skulls with a second stomach so we could pack away extra hot dogs without getting a big gut. But God wanted us to think and plan and try to work things out. We just need to remember that God has the *best* plans and his plans will prevail (win in the end).

What are your plans? Do you wanna get a job to earn cash or make some team or go on an outing? Then plan and work to make it happen. Just remember, you're not in control of all the factors, so although you should do your best,

there's no guarantee things will work out the way you planned.

While you're getting excited about dreams and plans, remember that God's the best planner of all, and whatever *he* wants to happen is what's going to happen. Yes, you need to work hard to try to figure things out, but you also need to pray and ask God to show you his will. Ask him to work with your brain and help you get it right. Even if he doesn't show you, ask him to work things out.

God gave you a brain because he figured you'd need it, so fire the thing up and use it. But being truly smart means letting God help you make the best plans come true.

Devotion #35
LIBRARIES AND LEARNING

A Jew named Apollos, a native of Alexandria, ... was a learned man, with a thorough knowledge of the Scriptures.

— Acts 18:24

Back in Roman times, the city of Alexandria, in Egypt, had the largest library on this planet. Like, half a million scrolls and books! It was a major center for learning. Some of the deepest thinkers went there to study and learn — and maybe to get lost in the dusty back aisles a few times. Apollos was one of those learned men. He not only learned math and science and history, but he also knew the Bible back to front and inside out.

Some boys today devour books — especially comic books and manga — but

they know practically nothing about the Bible. That's because they read those other books (sometimes over and over again), but when it comes to the Scriptures, they depend on adults to tell them the stories. Or they just get a bit of the action by reading Bible storybooks with big, bright pictures.

How did Apollos get his huge download of knowledge? He wasn't wandering along when a thousand books collapsed on him and he woke up smart. No. He *read* every word in all those books. If you wanna learn, you need to read. And while you're reading away, read your Bible, not just comics or storybooks. If you want the really good stuff, you gotta dive into the Good Book itself.

Having someone feed you spiritual food is okay when you're little, but when you get older, you gotta crack open the Bible and feed yourself.

Devotion #36
CHILDISH THINKING

Brothers, stop thinking like children.
— 1 Corinthians 14:20

The apostle Paul had just finished writing the following words: "When I was a child, I talked like a child, I thought like a child. I reasoned like a child. When I became a man, I put childish ways behind me" (1 Corinthians 13:11). Then he tells all of us to do the same — to "stop thinking like children." It's okay to think like a little kid if you are one. But when you grow up, it's time to move up a few levels in the game.

If you whine over your breakfast cereal, your older brother might say, "C'mon. Act your age!" Or maybe you gross everyone out by mining boogers in public, and some girl groans, "Oooo,

sick! *Grow up!*" (Okay, you had that one coming.)
But sometimes, for no reason, some kid insults you
by saying that you still enjoy the purple dinosaur
show. But Paul wasn't trying to insult anyone. He was
just reminding people not to slip back into childish
thinking.

You can tell you're growing up when you stop
thinking childish thoughts. That doesn't mean you're
suddenly superserious and you never look at a toy
again. You stop childish thinking when you start
considering other people's needs, not just yours. You
don't goof off when it's time to work, and you're not
easily offended or quick to quarrel. Those are all signs
of maturing.

You can still have plenty of fun. Growing up
just means your definition of fun changes. Instead of
enjoying childish play and purple dinosaurs, you're on
the next level.

devotion #37

PETE TAKES THE HEAT

The circumcised believers criticized him ...
Peter began and explained everything to them
precisely as it had happened.

— Acts 11:2 – 4

Yup, Peter's in trouble ... again. This is the
same disciple who rebuked Jesus. This is the
guy who hacked off someone's ear with his
sword. This is Peter, who denied that he even
knew Jesus. Now he's in trouble again. So
what's new? Wait! This time Pete's taking
heat for doing good. He'd been preaching
the gospel to Gentiles (non-Jews), a big no-
no to some Jewish Christians. After Pete
explained himself, they believed him and
everything was cool.

It's easy for us to believe that
Peter was right this time around; we're

reading the story two thousand years later. But it wasn't clear for folks back then, so at first they jumped all over him. What about you? If some kid's goofed up in the past, are you quick to presume him guilty before he has a chance to open his mouth? Don't. "He who answers before listening—that is his folly and his shame" (Proverbs 18:13).

Sure, you get an idea what to expect from people because of their past track record, but guess what! People can change. And they *do* change, all the time. So if you don't want to put your foot in your mouth—or theirs—let others explain. Afterward, if you still think they goofed up, at least you'll know you gave them a chance to tell their story.

Don't criticize people before you even hear them out. Peter changed. Others can change too. Give them a chance.

Devotion #38
DOG GODS AND COPYCATS

Solomon's wisdom was greater than . . .
all the wisdom of Egypt.

— 1 Kings 4:30

At times you'll hear people talk about "the wisdom of ancient Egypt." Well, the Egyptians *were* plenty smart. When it came to planting crops, running cities, doing math, keeping detailed records, and learning the lessons of history, the Egyptians were famous for their wisdom. Some of their wise men wrote practical advice similar to what Solomon wrote in the book of Proverbs. But Solomon was wisest of all.

Sad to say, however, Egyptians worshiped scores of idols, and a lot of their "wisdom" included dirges to dog-headed gods, discussions on how dung beetles created the world, and please-don't-eat-

me prayers to crocodiles. So be careful. If someone hands you the Egyptian *Book of the Dead* and says, "Hey, dude, check out the ancient wisdom of Egypt," tell 'im you don't dig dead-dog dudes or the mumbling of mummies.

Why try to sift through Egyptian myths when you can read the clear, inspired sayings of Solomon right in the Bible? And while you're at it, get a load of the ancient wisdom in the Psalms. These books tell you how to live and love God and your fellow man. They give you hope! And read the Gospels. You can find life — eternal life — in the Bible, but how can you find life in the *Book of the Dead*?

Rap: Da dog god's dead! Who cares what he said? King Sol said it best. Who cares about da rest? I can dig King Tut, but I don't dig no mutt. Leave da dog gods alone. Dey be buried with der bones.

devotion #39
FINDING OUT COOL STUFF

I, Daniel, understood from the Scriptures . . .
that the desolation of Jerusalem
would last seventy years.

— Daniel 9:2

Daniel's sitting in Babylon where his people
are prisoners. Meanwhile, his hometown of
Jerusalem is desolate (in ruins). Daniel's
reading the book of Jeremiah and comes
to the part that says the Jews will be
prisoners seventy years in Babylon
(Jeremiah 25:11 – 12). That catches
Daniel's attention! He reads a little
further, and his eyes nearly pop out!
When the seventy years are up,
guess what? The Jews will return to
Jerusalem (Jeremiah 29:10). Daniel's

thinking, "Good thing I read this! Now I know what's gonna happen!"

Maybe you feel the Bible's so deep that only adults can get stuff out of it, or that it's just full of poetry and history. No, God's Word is packed full of stuff for all ages. In fact, that's why Zondervan published a special Bible for tween boys called the *Boy's Bible*. It zeros in on all the gross, funny, and amazing stuff that boys your age are interested in.

Be glad if your parents require you to read a couple of Bible chapters every day. Sure, some parts won't be exploding with excitement and adventure, but you're bound to run across helpful info and find answers to your questions. There'll also be days where you're reading along and, like Daniel, you'll stumble across some completely mind-boggling facts.

You find out cool stuff when you study the Bible. You might not find it the first day, or even the second. But keep reading, and you'll hit pay dirt.

Devotion #40
FLAT FLATTERY

Such people are not serving our Lord Christ ... By smooth talk and flattery they deceive the minds of naive people.

— Romans 16:18

Paul warned Christians in Rome to watch out for those who came teaching a different message than he'd taught them. These Christians had heard the truth, but now false teachers were moving in and dumping weird stuff on them. These false teachers knew how to deceive the naive (people who are not very wise about the world). How? They used flattery and said stuff like, "Oh, you're so special! That's why I'm telling you this secret, special stuff."

There are smooth-talking deceivers around today too. If someone said to you, "The Bible doesn't say such-and-such is wrong," you might say, "Cool! I've always wanted to do that!" Another false teacher may be in the form of popular books and movies. If some author writes a book telling outrageous lies about Jesus — that he was a magician or that he never died on the cross — the book becomes a bestseller.

The best way to avoid being tricked by smooth talkers is to read your Bible. Know what it says and doesn't say. That way you won't believe every fast-talking trickster who makes a false claim. Of course, sometimes you won't know where in the Bible to find an answer, so ask your parents or your pastor. They've usually spent years studying it. They'll know.

If some smooth talker tries scrambling your brain by telling you weird stuff about the Bible, tell him you're not in the baloney-buying business. Then avoid him.

Devotion #41
KNOW BETTER THAN GOD? NOT!

"You acted foolishly," Samuel said. *"You have not kept the command the LORD your God gave you."*

— 1 Samuel 13:13

God had given King Saul *verrry* clear instructions. Saul was to gather his army and wait. Seven days later, the prophet Samuel would arrive, sacrifice to God, and then Saul and his army could battle the Philistines. Samuel had spelled out exactly what to do, but when day seven rolled around and Samuel didn't show up immediately, Saul grabbed the nearest knife and made the sacrifice himself. He wasn't supposed to! Seconds after he finished, Samuel showed up.

Saul wasn't the only willful guy in the history of this planet to think

that he had a better idea than God. For thousands of centuries since Saul, people have continued making the same kinds of boneheaded mistakes. God says something in his Word, but it seems to make no sense, so people ignore it. Or they say, "Times have changed. God doesn't still expect me to love my enemies." *Bwaaaaaap!* Wrong answer.

God's Word doesn't always tell us *exactly* what to do. God gave us brains, and he intended for us to use them. So you'll do well to put on your thinking cap and figure out what to do. The problem comes when God's Word tells you *exactly* what to do and you still try to "figure things out." That's where you end up with *Saul*-utions instead of solutions.

Don't pull a Saul and act foolishly. Use your brain and choose to do what God says to do. That's being really smart.

Devotion #42
LOVE YOURSELF? PROVE IT!

He who gets wisdom loves his own soul;
he who cherishes understanding prospers.
— Proverbs 19:8

For some guys, reading and learning and getting wisdom are a drag. School is *booorring*. They'd rather run off and join the circus, go rafting down the Mississippi with Tom Sawyer, or sail the Caribbean with a shipload of pirates — or at least do that on video games. Anything but school. Anything but reading the Bible and gaining godly wisdom.

But guess what? The Bible says that getting an education proves you love yourself. How so? If you wanna prove you love yourself, isn't it easier to just take five scoops of ice cream or spend all day at the swimming

pool? Isn't that self-love at its finest? (Or, like the advertisements say, "Buy Ploofie-doo shampoo 'cause you're worth it!")

No, that's all wrong. The way to prove you fear the Lord and love yourself is to get wisdom and understanding. Here's how it works: if you study hard in school, you'll get a better education, and you'll likely end up in a career that suits your God-given talents. You'll "prosper," or do well in life, and have true wisdom about practical situations.

Go for wisdom. Get understanding. Do the education thing, even if it's kind of boring at times. It proves you love yourself.

devotion #43

BAD BOY'S GOOD ADVICE

Now go out and encourage your men . . .
If you don't go out, not a man will be left
with you by nightfall.

— 2 Samuel 19:7

When Absalom's army attacked David,
David's men risked their lives to defend him,
and Absalom died in the battle. Was David
relieved? No. He loved Absalom so much that
he wouldn't stop crying. David's men felt
awful, like they'd done something wrong.
General Joab often did stupid stuff, but *this*
time he wisely warned David he'd better get
out there and *thank* his men or they'd all
leave. Fortunately, David listened and the
kingdom was saved.

There are kids you don't like to
listen to, right? Some of them hassle

you all the time, so you don't want to say they're right even if they are right. Others are constantly doing stuff you think is dumb, so you've made up your mind that they aren't right about anything. Other kids like to lecture you and — even though they're usually right — they're so annoying that it's no fun listening to them.

If someone explains why you're wrong about something, don't tell yourself, "I can't admit *he's* right." It's foolish to be stubborn and refuse good advice. Remember Balaam: he refused to listen to his donkey, and it nearly cost his life! And hey, if David was willing to listen to a mess of a messenger like Joab, you're wise to do the same.

Even if someone's way of saying stuff stinks, it's still worth listening to him if he happens to be right.

devotion #44
TOP CAMEL MAN

Obil the Ishmaelite was in charge
of the camels.

— 1 Chronicles 27:30

Obil was a camel expert, and King David had
camels — *lots* of them! Go figure. His kingdom
stretched from Egypt to the Euphrates River.
Want trade caravans? Gotta have camels. So who
should David put in charge of every camel in the
kingdom? One name shot to the top of the list:
Obil the Ishmaelite. He wasn't an Israelite,
true — he was an Arab — but Obil knew the
most about camels, and the guy who was
best at the job got the job.

If you feel different from other kids,
don't sweat it. Millions of families have
moved to America from other countries to

find a better life in — *ta da!* — the Land of Opportunity, where your talents and abilities matter more than where you came from. Maybe that's you. Or maybe that's some of your friends. It's cool to be different, but sometimes you wonder, *Yeah, but will I fit in? Will I succeed?* Look at Obil.

Or maybe your parents weren't immigrants. Maybe your great-great-great-grandfather was the first, famous, real McCoy to leap off the *Mayflower*, climb up on Plymouth Rock, and beat his chest. But still, that was *him*. You're *you*. Maybe you feel like you're nobody special and wonder if you'll succeed in life when you grow up. The answer to that is easy: study hard, and you can find your unique talent.

Want to succeed in your future career? Take a tip from Obil: know your stuff inside out, and you'll shoot up to the top of the class.

Devotion #45
JUNK TALK

Do not let any unwholesome talk come out of your mouths, but only what is helpful for building others up according to their needs.

— Ephesians 4:29

The opposite of wholesome, healthy food is unwholesome food, or *junk* food. Well, the opposite of wholesome talk is junk talk. Want to know what that is? Think of some kid swearing, acting out-of-control foolish, or trash-talking someone else. That's what the Bible means when it says don't let unwholesome talk come out of your mouth.

Some people don't think before they speak. They just blab whatever pops into their mind — potty humor, sick jokes, or whatever. As long as it's

good for a laugh, they don't care who they gross out. It doesn't matter if it builds someone up and encourages that person or knocks them down and discourages them. And sure enough, junk talk drags everyone down.

That's why it's smart to think before you speak. Ask yourself, "What does this person need to hear?" Then say those things. That doesn't mean pouring on false compliments. Just be careful what you say. If you don't care for something, look for something descriptive to say that isn't hurtful. Like if your grandmother asks what you think of her new hairdo, don't reply, "Weird! It looks like gray cotton candy." Just say, "It has nice curls." Or if your friend asks what you think of his drawing, stop yourself from blurting out, "It reeks." Tell him what parts you like and offer a suggestion if he needs it.

When you think of other people's feelings before you speak, that's wisdom kicking in. Sometimes you can't help it if foolish thoughts pop into your mind. Just don't let them come out of your mouth.

devotion #46
AVOID CAUSING GRIEF

Early the next morning Abraham
took some food and a skin of water
and gave them to Hagar ... then
sent her off with the boy.

— Genesis 21:14

When God told Abraham to send Hagar
and Ishmael away, it was hard on Abraham
because he really loved Ishmael. But he
obeyed God and did it. Unfortunately, Abe
didn't think things through and *forgot* to send
a couple of camels loaded down with gold and
silver and food and water. He sent them out
with only a bit of food and a water jug.
They nearly died in the desert!

Ever slipped up like that? You're
supposed to feed your younger brother

while your mom's out and you forget — and as soon as Mom walks in the door, he tells her that he's starving. Or your mom says to give your hamster away, so you just leave the cage on the curb with a "Free" sign on it.

If your mom tells you to take care of your brothers or sisters, stop playing video games long enough to see that they get lunch. You'll avoid causing others grief. And about hamsters: if you own one, either take care of the pitiful little fuzz ball or find someone who will. If you give it away, include the hamster food. You don't need that stuff, right? The hamster does.

Abraham slipped up, but fortunately God performed a miracle and took care of Hagar and Ishmael. But don't expect God to cover for *you*: if you're supposed to care for people or pets, think about it and do it.

devotion #47
A SENSE OF TIMING

The wise heart will know the proper time and
procedure. For there is a proper time
and procedure for every matter.

— Ecclesiastes 8:5 – 6

It's great if you know the solution to a
problem. But just having knowledge is not good
enough. You also need wisdom on the best way to
use your smarts. There's also a good time to bring
things up . . . and *really bad times* to do it. If you
pack these two facts into your brain, the Bible
says you'll be wise.

For example, if you wanna tell
your friend how to get rid of a wart, you
don't shout it out when he's about to
give a speech to the class. There's also
a procedure. With a lot of things in life,

you need to fill out these forms first, pick a number, and then wait to be called. With your friends, you don't need to fill out a Wart Form, but smart "time and procedure" would be to take him aside privately and tell him after his speech.

It's the same with asking your mom if you can go over to a friend's house. Don't just burst through the door after school and blurt it out — especially if she's talking to her long-lost aunt Harriet on the phone, the spaghetti sauce is boiling over, and a bowl just broke. You'll probably get no for an answer just because of your incredibly bad timing.

Want good results? Before you say something, ask yourself, "Is this a good time?" and "Is this the right way to go about it?"

devotion #48

FEELING DUMB?

I am the most ignorant of men; I do not
have a man's understanding. I have
not learned wisdom, nor have I
knowledge of the Holy One.

— Proverbs 30:2 – 3

One day a dude named Agur was
having a chat with his pals Ithiel and
Ucal, and he told them, "I am the most
ignorant of men; I do not have a man's
understanding." You notice they didn't
argue, "C'mon, Agur! Don't be so hard
on yourself. You're not *that* dumb."
Well, they should've! Agur may not
have been highly educated, but he
was smart about important stuff in life.

Ever feel dumb? That can happen if you compare yourself to kids with different talents than yours. When you hear some girl say she loves math, do you think, "Are you out of your mind?" You struggle to get a C or a C+, and she's pulling in A's like the stuff was easy? Things like that can discourage you. Maybe you start complaining about how dumb you are. Don't.

You can't be smart about everything. And just because some kid outshines you in math or science or history doesn't mean she's all that and more. Thank God for the smarts God *has* given you. Think about the stuff you're quick at — and not just school subjects. Of course, while you're at it, work hard to bring up your grades. But if you're already doing your best, don't beat yourself up.

Like Agur, you may feel you have not "learned wisdom," but God has made you smart in your own way. And anyone, whether they're a genius or not, can gain "knowledge of the Holy One" — God!

Devotion #49
TAKING CARE OF BUSINESS

"Your servant my husband is dead,
and you know that he revered the LORD.
But now his creditor is coming to take
my two boys as his slaves."

—2 Kings 4:1

This lady's husband was a prophet who honored God. Everybody knew that. Even the great prophet Elisha knew about him. But Mr. Prophet had borrowed a lot of money, and when he died his wife and kids were left with debts they couldn't pay. Now the bill collector was coming to grab the prophet's sons . . . as slaves! Fortunately, God performed a miracle and paid the debt, but that was a close call.

Now, the main lesson of this story is that God performed a miracle to deliver a faithful servant. Still, there's another lesson here, and that is you need to stop and think about your habits. Like, if you're always borrowing money and don't pay it back, after a while you'll owe so much you can't pay it back. Lose library books, and reading gets expensive. You won't get yourself sold into slavery, but you can cause yourself major pain.

The solution? Take care of details. Don't forget to pay your debts. God shouldn't have to perform a miracle to pay your bills for you — and most of the time he won't. He leaves it up to you to pay them, and if you don't, he lets you suffer the consequences. So change that habit and avoid grief.

Make sure you honor God like Mr. Prophet did. But also be smart and honor others by paying them what you owe them. You'll avoid lots of problems.

Devotion #50
SPECIAL TRAINING PLAN

"What is to be the rule for the boy's life and work?"

—Judges 13:12

One day an angel appeared and told a woman she'd have a son — and not just any son! This kid would be Samson, and he'd start delivering his people from the Philistines. This was going to be difficult for Samson's family — a lot was being asked of them — but instead of complaining, they were obedient to God and asked for a detailed plan.

It's cool being good at something, whether it's swimming or drawing or math or killing lions with your bare hands. It's cool if you realize at an early age that God has a special plan for your life. You do something you enjoy, you do it well, and

everyone applauds. Your parents want you to succeed, so when they notice you have talents — if they can afford it — they make you take lessons to develop those talents. The fun stuff's still fun, but it just became work too.

You may not be destined to be a lion slayer like Samson or a gold-medal athlete, but whatever your future holds — if you wanna become good at it — you need to go at it with a plan. You have to first of all determine to fulfill God's plan, then come up with a training regimen, and then discipline yourself and *work* that plan — even on days when it's more work than fun and you'd rather lie back on the couch and eat cream puffs and chips.

Be thankful if your talents and abilities show up early. And follow your special training plan — you'll get better at something you enjoy while you train for the future.

Devotion #51
TINY DETAILS, BIG SOLUTIONS

The Jebusites said to David, "You will not get in here" ... David said, "Anyone who conquers the Jebusites will have to use the water shaft."

— 2 Samuel 5:6, 8

When David became king of Israel, he wanted the city of Jebus for his capital. It sat on a steep hill, had high walls, and was the perfect fortress. Problem was, the Jebusites were already there. They mocked, "It's impossible for you to conquer us." Well, almost impossible. There was one way. David had grown up near Jebus, and he remembered a secret passage — the water shaft.

So he sent his soldiers climbing straight up that slippery tunnel into the city.

Sometimes you face difficult problems, and no matter what you try, nothing works. Maybe you're trying to get a TV remote to work and it won't. Or you've locked yourself out of the house and you can't get in. Or you need to study for a math test, but you left your math book in your school locker.

That's when you have to use creative solutions. You need to turn up the amps in your brain. At this point, remembering tiny but important details can be a real lifesaver. Like realizing that your toy car has the same kind of batteries as the remote, or remembering where your mom hid the spare house key, or getting permission to go study with a friend next door.

When you're facing an almost impossible problem, think outside the box. Ask God to show you any "water-shaft solutions" to the problem.

Devotion #52
HAPPY THOUGHTS VERSUS SICKNESS

A cheerful heart is good medicine, but
a crushed spirit dries up the bones.

— Proverbs 17:22

They didn't have a lot of medicines back in the days when Solomon wrote this, and they certainly had no X-rays or antibiotics. But Solomon realized a very important fact: "a crushed spirit dries up the bones." Not literally, of course. You won't turn into a fossil. But when you're seriously discouraged, it's like you have the energy drained right out of you. You don't feel like doing anything.

The thoughts that you think can affect your health. If you constantly worry, or you're bummed out day after day, or you have a negative, angry attitude, it can actually make you ill.

You don't need to have some bozo sneeze in your face to get sick. You can make yourself sick simply by thinking downer thoughts all the time. These are called psychosomatic (*psycho-so-mat-ik*) illnesses.

On the other hand, having a cheerful heart is like good medicine. Science has proved this. Hospital patients have sometimes improved their health by watching slapstick comedy shows and laughing their fool heads off. God designed it so that when you laugh, your brain releases healing chemicals into your bloodstream. And hey, trusting God and being happy because God loves you works wonders! Nehemiah 8:10 says, "The joy of the Lord is your strength."

Want to stay healthy and strong? The next time you're tempted to drag yourself around in a grumpy, growling mood, stay focused on positive, happy thoughts instead!

devotion #53

FILLED WITH SKILL

I have filled him with the Spirit of God,
with skill, ability and knowledge in all
kinds of crafts.

— Exodus 31:3

God gave Moses the exact designs for the
ark of the covenant and the Tent of Meeting.
(The ark was like a gold-covered treasure chest,
and the Tent of Meeting was like a huge, fancy
tent.) God also told Moses to build tables and
altars. Fine. Now Moses needed craftsmen to
actually build these things. Bezalel fit the bill
perfectly: he was smart, he knew how to
work with gold and silver and bronze, and
he was an excellent carpenter.

When God gives you abilities
and talents, you're naturally good at

something. Maybe you're a champ at sports, or you lead the pack with drawing or inventing complicated stuff out of Lego bricks. And skill? That's when you practice something so much that you become really, *really* good at it — like playing computer games or tossing a basketball. And of course, knowledge means learning all the ins and outs.

Okay, so God has given you natural abilities, and if you're willing to learn, you can add skill and knowledge to that. But check out that list again. Before God filled Bezalel with skill, ability, and knowledge, he *first* filled him with the Holy Spirit. This supernatural power connected him to God and gave his life purpose and meaning, and you gotta have that to truly succeed.

It's cool to have skills and abilities, but make sure — before anything else — that you ask God to fill you with his Holy Spirit.

Devotion #54
TOTALLY INFINITE UNDERSTANDING

Great is our Lord and mighty in power;
his understanding has no limit.

— Psalm 147:5

Not only is God the greatest muscle guy in the universe, but he knows absolutely everything about everything! His understanding has no limit — it is infinite! You think you're smart? Compared to God, you're like an ant with a brain the size of a bread crumb — a small bread crumb. Sometimes you're muddling through things, trying to solve problems that just won't go away. Or you're trying to understand stuff you just can't understand, and it gets so frustrating you feel like screaming or pounding the wall. It could be math, or it could be a problem in life. You think

and think, but you don't get an answer. You ask others what they think, but they don't know the solution either. So what do you do?

Pray. God can clue you in. Now, if you're praying for him to show you how to build a time machine, well, forget it. But if it's something you truly need to know, then you can expect an answer. Maybe you'll read the answer in the Bible, or maybe God will lead you to someone who knows. Or maybe you'll wake up one morning to find that God took care of it — even though you still don't understand what was happening.

God has the answers to everything. Obviously he must — there is no limit to his understanding. So tune in to him. It beats pounding the wall and banging up your knuckles.

devotion #55
WORTH GETTING ORGANIZED

*"What you are doing is not good.
You and these people ... will only
wear yourselves out. The work is
too heavy for you."*

— *Exodus 18:17 – 18*

After Moses led the Israelites out of Egypt,
everyone in camp came running to him with
their questions and wanted him to settle their
quarrels. So he did. Crowds stood around
from morning to evening, day after day, while
Moses sat there listening and judging. Both
Moses and the people were wiped out at
the end of each day. Moses' father-in-law
gave him some good advice: let other
guys handle the easy cases; you just
listen to the tough ones.

You can wear yourself out by trying to do the whole job by yourself. Let's say you're building a snow fort and you don't want to let your little brother and sister help you because they'll "mess it up." You'll probably never finish the fort, and you *and* your brother and sister will be frustrated. What also won't work is if you're doing a school project with friends but you insist on doing the whole thing yourself.

You have to learn to share the job. Give part of the work to other people and let them help you. To do that, you need to *trust* other people. Sure, you may think they can't do as good a job as you, but you won't do a great job either if you collapse on the floor exhausted.

It paid for Moses to get organized. Learn from him and don't try to do the whole job yourself. Work smarter, not harder.

Devotion #56
WISDOM AND WRINKLES

Rehoboam rejected the advice the elders gave him and consulted the young men who had grown up with him.

— 1 Kings 12:8

Rehoboam was a young guy when he became king. The Israelites said, "Make our lives easier! Lower the taxes!" So Rehoboam checked with his counselors about that. The wise old elders said yes, that was definitely a good thing to do. But Rehoboam dumped their advice and asked his young pals. They said, "Nah! *Increase* their taxes! Make their lives *harder*! That'll show 'em who's boss!" Rehoboam listened to his buds and lost most of the kingdom.

It's great when you're old enough to start thinking things through for

yourself and making your own decisions. It's a sign that you're growing up. But sometimes boys are *so* eager to prove they're independent, they deliberately ignore their parents' advice — even when it makes lots of sense. Yet if their friends advise them to ride their skateboard off a killer ramp, hey, they'll listen to *that*!

The rule of thumb is old people have lived long enough to get old because they didn't do dumb stuff like plunging off fifty-foot ramps. They learned what was smart and wise and made the most sense, and avoided doing some of the truly dumb things their friends told them to go for. Okay, your parents have done dumb stuff too, but they learned from it and it made them wiser.

It doesn't pay to ignore older people's advice. People with wrinkles really do have smarts.

devotion #57
TURNING ON THE TAP

Out of the overflow of the heart the mouth speaks. The good man brings good things out of the good stored up in him, and the evil man brings evil things out of the evil stored up in him.

— Matthew 12:34–35

You constantly take in sights and sounds and fill your mind with images. So when your tongue starts wagging, it draws on what's stored in your brain. If eighty percent of your brain cells are taken up by soccer knowledge, chances are high you'll talk about soccer. Sure, you can *try* to talk only about the knowledge that fills the

other twenty percent, but when you're full of a subject, it eventually flows out of your mouth.

Let's say you spend a lot of time playing violent video games and watching TV shows and movies where kids have sick attitudes and bad mouths. Do you really think that stuff will have no effect on the way you think and talk? Some kids argue, "I just like that stuff. I wouldn't actually talk about it or do it." Not at first, no, but eventually when your mind is used to it, yes, you will.

The flip side of the coin is that if you focus on good stuff, then good stuff will fill your mind so much that it will overflow and come out your mouth. That doesn't mean you should talk only about Bible verses or watch only VeggieTales. There's lots of good stuff out there. Have a good attitude about whatever you think or talk about — from sports to girls.

What you spend your time thinking about and reading and watching really does matter!

Devotion #58
GOD'S AMAZING UNIVERSE

Can you bind the beautiful Pleiades?

Can you loose the cords of Orion?

Can you ... lead out the Bear with its cubs?

Do you know the laws of the heavens?

—Job 38:31–33

These verses may sound like a rodeo roping event or some circus act, but God was actually talking about constellations, or groups of stars. Pleiades is a constellation that is also known as the seven sisters. Orion is also known as the hunter. Today "the Bear with its cubs" is known as *Ursa Major* (big bear) and *Ursa Minor* (little bear). No Goldilocks, sorry.

People have been studying stars for thousands of years, but scientists

still don't know everything about them. Do you know the laws of the heavens? No, chances are you didn't even know Pleiades and Orion existed. Like most people, you don't know how black holes suck in stars like slushies. You don't know why gravity pulls the way it does. (It works, sure, but according to scientists' calculations, it should be a lot stronger.)

Scientists are beginning to think now that the reason gravity's not stronger is because it exists in another dimension, and only a little bit of it leaks into our physical universe. (Seriously, they *really* think that!) Obviously, these scientists are making a hypothesis. They are still trying to fully understand stuff like how gravity works. God knows all the laws of the heavens! Well, he should. He invented them.

Since God created all the laws of the universe, imagine how smart he is! That's a good reason to trust what he says in the Bible.

Devotion #59

IMPRESSED HEARTS

These commandments that I give you today are to be upon your hearts. Impress them on your children.

— Deuteronomy 6:6 – 7

When God gave the Israelites the Ten Commandments (and all the other commands), he didn't just want his people to know about them. He wanted them to really, really know them. They had to have God's commands so deep in their hearts, they practically memorized them and obeyed them quickly and easily. Then they were supposed to impress them on their kids' hearts.

Speaking of *impressing*, ever take one of those plastic stamp thingies and press it on play dough? It leaves an

impression. That's about how God wants his Word to be in your heart. If your parents or Sunday school teachers make you memorize Bible verses, they're helping get God's Word impressed in your heart. As David said, "I have hidden your word in my heart that I might not sin against you" (Psalm 119:11).

It may sometimes seem like a chore and a bore if your mom and dad constantly teach you guidelines and laws, quote Bible verses to you, and write out lists of your duties. But that's what parents are supposed to do, because doing these things helps you in life. That was your most basic education before you even started going to school, and it'll continue to be a part of your learning curve as long as you're growing up.

When you really know God's commands and they're impressed deep on your heart — then you're more likely to live by them. And that's the idea.

Devotion #60
GETTING A SECOND OPINION

Make plans by seeking advice;
if you wage war, obtain guidance.
— Proverbs 20:18

When Solomon said, "Make plans by seeking advice," he meant get lots of good advice from people who've been there, done that, and lived to tell the tale. Then finalize your plans. When he says, "If you wage war, obtain guidance," he isn't talking about a snowball battle. He's advising kings not to just send soldiers charging into battle without a plan, but to first sit down with wise old warriors and let them explain how to do things.

When you have to do something you've never done before — like planning a camping trip

or dogsledding across Antarctica — seek advice. Don't say, "Man, this is such a no-brainer, I'm going to just do it." You could end up fighting mosquitoes while you set up a tent in a swamp in the pouring rain at midnight. Or your dog team could be ambushed by giant killer penguins at the South Pole. (Just kidding!)

Other people may have experience to share; they've done it before and know what to do and what not to do. They can help you figure out the best way to do things. (Or they may warn you not to try it at all.) They may know how to put up a tent so it doesn't fill up with thirsty mosquitoes and sink in the swamp. Or they may know where to buy sled dogs.

Even if you've done something before, hey, situations change, so check things out each time.

Devotion #61
WISDOM VERSUS BOOK LEARNING

"How did this man get such learning without having studied?"

—John 7:15

Jewish boys went to school in Jesus' day, but their education was mostly memorizing the laws of Moses, discussing the laws' details, and learning to read and write. And that was it. If a young guy wanted more education, he had to find a teacher (rabbi) and study under him. Jesus didn't do that. When he finished school, he went to work full-time as a carpenter. So where did he get his massive wisdom and learning? From God, his Father!

Unless your family's plane crashed on a tropical island and all you learned while growing up was how to wrestle sharks and climb coconut palms,

chances are you'll get a decent education. But you'd be surprised at how many high-school graduates don't know important stuff like how to use a credit card wisely, how to take care of a car, how to do their laundry, and how to relate to others. Some are especially clueless when it comes to spiritual stuff.

You can learn about credit cards, cars, and laundry simply by living life. But when it comes to the important spiritual stuff, you need to really love God, spend time with him, and learn from him. You can go to Bible school — sure, that'll help a lot — but it's more important to read your Bible yourself and have a relationship with God.

God can give you wisdom, so pray and ask him to start giving you the kind of deep wisdom you can't learn from just reading textbooks.

Devotion #62
CAFETERIA-STYLE EXPERTS

They want to be teachers of the law, but they do not know what they are talking about or what they so confidently affirm.

— 1 Timothy 1:7

In Paul's day, some guys got odd ideas in their heads . . . then read the Scriptures to find verses to prove their theories. Problem was, they hadn't studied the Bible, so they didn't understand what it was really saying. They just went along cafeteria-style, picking this verse and that. They were confidently affirming stuff — meaning they boasted and insisted they were right — but they didn't have a clue *what* they were talking about.

People do the same thing today. For example, some people think the Bible isn't talking about God and his angels, but about aliens and UFOs. Even though there's *nothing* in the Bible about this, they read the entire book with that idea stuck in their brain. They read Ezekiel's description of God's throne and say, "Yup! That's a flying saucer if I ever saw one!" They read, "Aliens will shepherd your flocks" (Isaiah 61:5) and scream, "That proves it!"

This is called having selective hearing — choosing information cafeteria-style. For the record, God's throne is God the Father's throne, not some mother ship. The angels are not actually little green men; they're angels. And the aliens that guarded the Israelites' fluffy little sheep were actually *foreigners*, not E.T.

Before you start spreading alien ideas around, give the Bible an honest reading. Take off the rose-colored glasses — in this case, the little green glasses — and see what it's really saying.

Devotion #63
IT PAYS TO LISTEN

If you have anything to say, answer me ... But if not, then listen to me; be silent, and I will teach you wisdom.

—Job 33:32 – 33

When Job suffered a disaster, his friends took turns trying to figure out why God had let such bad things happen to him. The first three pals basically told Job, "God's punishing you." Finally it was Elihu's turn, and fortunately, Elihu was wiser. Now, Job had argued back to the other three guys, and Elihu had heard all of Job's explanations. Elihu was willing to listen if Job had anything new to say, but he also wanted Job to pay attention when *he* was talking.

You've probably noticed that it bugs your teacher or coach — or even your friends — if they're trying to teach you something or explain something and you keep interrupting, saying, "Yeah, yeah. I *know* that. I know. I know." If someone's trying to explain something to you, one of the surest signs that you're not listening — and not *wanting* to listen — is if you're talking back.

If you have something to say or need to explain something, by all means say it. But when your parents have let you say your piece, then open your ears to what they have to say. Even if you already know *some* of what they're telling you, respect them by listening. They'll probably say something you really need to hear.

There is a time to talk and explain your side of things. But when it's time to listen, then listen. You'll learn stuff and end up wiser.

devotion #64
TRUTH VERSUS MYTH

They will gather around them a great number of teachers to say what their itching ears want to hear. They will turn their ears away from the truth and turn aside to myths.

— 2 Timothy 4:3-4

In Paul's day, some intellectual people liked the idea of a wise teacher named Jesus, but they freaked when Paul said that Jesus saved us by dying for our sins and then coming back to life. To them, that was too easy. They rejected the gospel and began inventing all kinds of complicated myths (made-up stories) about Jesus.

Today too, many people are "itchy" for something different. When their ears start itching like crazy, they

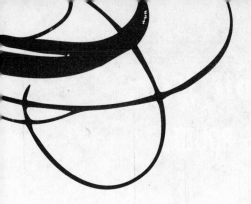

figure the best way to scratch them is to stuff them full of interesting, bizarre theories. So they gather busloads of teachers and go gaga over old false books like the Gospel of Judas. (According to that so-called gospel, Judas was a hero for betraying Jesus!)

If you think those teachers with their myths are out to lunch, you've got that one right! The simple truth beats mixed-up myths any day. So how do you avoid swallowing interesting lies? By knowing what the Bible actually says about Jesus and by living for the truth. That way, when strange Bible teachers come along, your ears won't be itchy for their lies.

These days, lots of people turn their ears away from the truth because they don't want to hear it. Don't you do that. Read your Bible and listen to godly teachers.

Devotion #65

UNREASONABLE DOUBTS

But they did not believe
the women, because their words
seemed to them like nonsense.

—Luke 24:11

When some women went to Jesus' tomb and found his body was missing, angels informed them Jesus had risen from the dead. The women ran and told the apostles, but the men didn't believe them. Then Jesus appeared and rebuked them for thinking it was nonsense. You can understand the apostles' doubts. People didn't rise from the dead every day. So why did Jesus rebuke them? 'Cause hey, guys, he only told you half a dozen times that he'd be crucified and then rise from the dead!

Sometimes doubts are good, like if someone claims they've discovered the Loch Ness monster or the remains of Atlantis. You *should* be suspicious. You *should* doubt, because people have lied about that before. In 1922 a scientist found a fossil tooth in Nebraska and announced it was from the missing link. Turns out it was a tooth from a wild pig! *Ooops!* You learn what to expect from certain people.

Jesus' disciples should have believed because he'd always told the truth in the past. Yet when he rose from the dead, it caught them totally by surprise. In this case, having doubts didn't show how *well* their brains were working. All it showed was that they hadn't been paying attention when Jesus was talking. Either that or they had bad memories.

When someone tells you something astonishing, ask questions. Some doubts are reasonable. Just remember that other doubts are unreasonable. Ditch those doubts!

Devotion #66
DEAD FRED AND MADAME MAMBA

When men tell you to consult mediums and spiritists, who whisper and mutter, should not a people inquire of their God? Why consult the dead on behalf of the living?

— Isaiah 8:19

A *medium* is a person who claims she can give you supernatural wisdom because the departed spirit of your dead uncle Fred just entered her and possessed her and is talking through her mouth. Spooky, huh? A *spiritist* is anyone who claims to have the power to talk to spirits of the dead. The Bible warns against this weirdness.

You may have heard of people who phone mediums with names like the Mysterious Madame Mamba. Why do they do it? Well, they have so little faith in God that they're not content to pray to him and trust him with their future. So they hope old Uncle Fred's spirit is floating around with nothing better to do than advise them on who to fall in love with, how to spend their money, etc.

Don't do it. Madame Mambas are extremely expensive, and on top of that, they're faking it. Yup, they're lying. Uncle Fred is either in heaven or the other place. He's not popping into the brain of some medium. Even if Uncle Fred were around, he wouldn't have any inside scoop.

Why talk to the dead? What do the dead know? You're a lot smarter and a *lot* better off praying and asking God and reading in the Bible about stuff.

Devotion #67
THE RIGHT KIND OF WISDOM

*I want you to be wise about what
is good, and innocent about what is evil.*

— Romans 16:19

Sometimes you hear an adult tell his life story and talk about the stuff he was into before he became a Christian. Maybe he talks about drinking, taking drugs, riding with a biker gang, or fighting in prison. You think, "Huh, that sounds exciting." Don't kid yourself. If these guys could do it over, there's no way they'd wallow in the pig mud again.

A lot of kids today have things mixed up. Instead of being wise about what is good and innocent about what is evil, they know nearly *nothing* about what is good but are very well informed about evil. Ask them Bible questions, and they

draw blanks. But ask them about the newest shoot-'em-dead video game, and they rattle off the names of all the characters and how much power each of their weapons has.

You become "wise about what is good" when you read your Bible and hang around with godly people. You stay "innocent about what is evil" by refusing to watch bad movies, by not playing dark video games, and by steering away from drugs. Now, you may feel sometimes that good stuff is boring — it's more exciting to play games rated for teens than to sit in church. But seeing someone's life changed by a kind act or watching your neighborhood improve by cleaning up a park is pretty exciting.

There's a lot of dark stuff around today, and it takes a deliberate choice to avoid it. You have to keep choosing good, not evil, day after day.

Devotion #68
WEREN'T BORN YESTERDAY?

Ask the former generations and find out what their fathers learned, for we were born only yesterday and know nothing.

— Job 8:8 – 9

Ever had someone tell you something really basic, and you reply, "Hey, I wasn't born yesterday!"? Well, *this* dude Bildad, who said, "We were born only yesterday," was at least fifty years old — and he and his friends were smart. Yet Bildad still felt like they'd only been born yesterday compared to the really wise old people of the previous generations. Mind you, he was exaggerating a *bit* when he said they knew nothing. (Otherwise, how would they even know how to talk?)

By the time you're ten, eleven, or twelve years old, you know quite a bit. You've spent years studying stuff in school, you've read books, watched TV, and even learned a couple of things from talking to other kids. Since you can play complex video games that your parents are hopeless at, you realize that you know more than Mom and Dad about *some* things.

Okay, so you may know video games, but life is a lot bigger than a fast thumb and robot-zapping reflexes. When it comes to the serious things of life — what works and what doesn't, hard-earned experiences, and just overall knowledge — your parents have like a twenty- or thirty-year head start. Watching a one-hour documentary on baboons or knowing how to feed a virtual pet helps, but it won't make you an instant expert on life.

Ask the older generation. Find out what your father learned. You might be surprised at just how much he knows.

Devotion #69
OKAY, YOU'VE GOT MY ATTENTION!

Then he said to his servants, "Look, Joab's field is next to mine ... Go and set it on fire."

—2 Samuel 14:30

General Joab was a powerful, feared man, but after Prince Absalom messed up and ran off to another land, Joab talked King David into bringing Absalom back. Now Absalom wanted Joab to do him *another* favor, but Joab ignored him. To get Joab's attention, Absalom told his servants to torch Joab's barley fields. Oh, yeah! *That* got Joab's attention, all right. A couple of years later, Joab killed Absalom.

Offending others to get yourself visible on their radar isn't wise. Sure, if you're mad, you feel like "teaching them a lesson." But those kinds of

stunts have a way of coming back at you. Like if your mom doesn't let you go on an outing, so you tromp your muddy shoes across the clean floor. Or you take it out on your sister and torment her. Yup, that'll get Mom's attention. It'll also get you grounded.

No matter how upset you feel when your friends don't do what you want them to do, don't lash out in anger at them. There are acceptable ways to let off steam without hurting yourself and others. Like praying, exercising, going for a walk, or pounding your pillow.

Think the consequences through before you do something rash. Sure, you're frustrated, but there are always smart solutions that beat dumb actions any day.

Devotion #70
KEEP THESE FACTS IN MIND

The officer ... said to the man of God, "Look, even if the LORD should open the floodgates of the heavens, could this happen?"

— 2 Kings 7:2

An army surrounded the city, and with no food coming in, there was a terrible famine. It lasted so long that people gave up hope. Then Elisha the prophet said that the next day they'd have tons of food. An officer snorted and said, "Impossible!" But it happened. You can understand the officer's being skeptical, but he had forgotten two facts: (a) Elisha was a prophet with a track record of fulfilled prophecies, and (b) God had performed *five* food miracles for Elisha before!

It's easy to get discouraged when you're in a tough situation for a long time and you've prayed and prayed and nothing's changed . . . yet. At first you wonder if God was listening. Then you think about it and realize, "Well, he's God! Of course he heard me!" Then you wonder why he doesn't answer, and you're tempted to either give up on prayer or get mad at God.

When you're discouraged, don't overlook important facts that can give you hope. Here are the facts: the Bible is true, God answers in his own way and time, and trusting him has worked before. Often you need to trust even though you don't understand why things are taking so long. But the reason you *can* trust is because you know that God has delivered in the past.

When you're tempted to doubt that God cares, or think he doesn't have the power to change things, remember his track record and think again!

devotion #71
SAUNA ROOM SCHOOL

He took the disciples with him
and had discussions daily in the lecture
hall of Tyrannus. This went on for two years.

— Acts 19:9 – 10

One time the apostle Paul had no place to teach new Christians, so professor Tyrannus (not Tyrannosaurus Rex) was kind enough to let him use his lecture hall. There was, um, one downside. Tyrannus taught in the cool morning hours. Paul had the schoolroom during the afternoon. The hall was probably free — but hot. This was in ancient Turkey, and the Christians probably felt like they were turkeys baking in an oven. It was like going to school in a sauna.

Unless your class has air-conditioning and an ice-cream break

every hour, you probably can relate to this. When you're sitting in class or Sunday school in the summer heat — and the windows are open but it's not helping — maybe you wish you were somewhere else — like, at the waterslides. The teacher's talking, but your body's approaching meltdown, and your mind is barely there.

What's the solution? Well, if you're gonna get anything out of the class, you have to tune out the heat, turn off the daydreams, and get in the zone mentally. You do that by remembering *why* you're there. You're in Sunday school to learn about Jesus, the most powerful guy in the universe. You're in school because a good education means a better life.

Just how badly do you want to learn? When school is boring or your classroom is sweltering, remember Paul and the sweating Christians. They stuck it out for two years to learn about God. Stick it out. It's worth it.

Devotion #72

OPEN EARS, OPEN MIND

Let the wise listen and add to their learning.

— Proverbs 1:5

When you're really into something, you just devour information about it — whether it's baseball or fishing or dirt biking or video games. Learning comes easy. Your mind's open, your ears are tuned in, and — like a starving piranha — you gulp down new facts because you're *interested* in more. When you already have lots of learning, and you add to what you know, you're at the top of your game.

One guy in the New Testament was named Philologus, which means "lover of learning." We don't know if Phil lived up to his name, but obviously

his mom and dad had high hopes for him. Now, any kid is naturally gonna find some subjects interesting and other subjects boring. But the way life's set up, you can't just focus on video games and skateboarding and let everything else slide. You need to learn the "boring" stuff too.

Even if you're not keen on math, it pays to know how to walk into a store, buy a "brain freeze," and walk back out again with the correct change. So how do you learn stuff when you're not that interested? By listening. By making yourself focus and refusing to let your mind daydream. By not passing drawings around the class or bouncing spitballs off some kid's head. Whatever you're studying, give it your attention.

Want to learn stuff? Or at least *need* to learn stuff? Then listen when the teacher's mouth is moving. There'll be time for skateboarding and computer games afterward.

Devotion #73

EXTREME RESEARCH

They searched in the archives stored
in the treasury at Babylon. A scroll was
found in the citadel of Ecbatana
in the province of Media.

— Ezra 6:1 – 2

Way back when the Persians were ruling the land, the Jews began to rebuild their temple. The local Persian official asked, "Um, guys. Do you have permission to do that?" The Jews told him, "Sure we do. Check your records." So the official had the librarians in Babylon search through the documents. They found nothing. Did they give up? Nope. They kept at it and finally tracked the document down in Ecbatana — three hundred miles away!

These days it's a lot easier to find facts. There's Google and a dozen other search engines that blitz through the Internet to supply you with information. But researching can still be work — especially if you don't have the right search words, or you have to jog to the library and check through tons of books. Things are so easy these days that when something's just a bit hard, you can be tempted to throw up your hands and give up.

The key to doing great research — even looking for a pair of socks — is to make up your mind that you're not gonna give up if you don't succeed instantly. Stick to it. Time and time again, victory comes to those who simply refuse to give up.

Keep at it when you have to dig out facts. After all, it's not like someone's making you ride a camel three hundred miles to Ecbatana to hunt down some scroll.

devotion #74
TESTED WITH HARD QUESTIONS

When the queen of Sheba heard about the fame of Solomon ... she came to test him with hard questions ... Solomon answered all her questions.

— 1 Kings 10:1, 3

These verses don't mean that the queen of Sheba gave Solomon a killer math test. No, she did a lot of deep thinking and wasn't satisfied with the answers her wise men gave, so she was saving up a list of tough questions. When she heard how wise Solomon was, she hopped on her camel and rode a thousand miles north to Jerusalem to quiz him. Some of her questions must've been humdingers. No sweat. Solomon had the answers.

Ms. Sheba wasn't asking Solomon trivia questions, either. She was asking deep stuff like, "Why are we on earth?" and "Why do good people die?" (the kind of questions people still ask today). Well, as smart as Solomon was, an even wiser person came along — Jesus! Luke 11:31 says, "The Queen of the South . . . came from the ends of the earth to listen to Solomon's wisdom, and now one greater than Solomon is here."

Solomon's answers to the queen's questions are lost, but, fortunately, some guy with a pen was handy when Jesus was talking, so his wisdom was written down and is recorded in the Gospels. This is great news when you consider that Jesus answered the very toughest questions of all. That's why it's important to read the Gospels.

It's cool to ask hard, deep questions. That's how you get answers. And there *are* answers. Check out the Bible today.

Devotion #75
UNDERSTANDING AND TRUSTING

Trust in the LORD with all your heart and
lean not on your own understanding.

— Proverbs 3:5

Does God think that understanding stuff is important? Oh, yeah! The Bible says that no matter how much it costs, get knowledge and get understanding. Getting knowledge is what God made a busy brain for. God also wants you to *use* that knowledge. But here the Bible says to "lean *not* on your own understanding," but lean on God and trust him instead. *Huh?*

Some people misunderstand this verse and think it means they should just drift through life without thinking things through or preparing or asking important questions:

"Have you studied for tomorrow's science test?"

"No, I don't wanna lean on my own understanding."

"Do you understand how to fix your bike?"

"No, God must not want me to ride it."

"Did you prepare for the dangers you'll face in Death Swamp?"

"No, I'm just trusting God."

So what does this verse mean? When God has *already* given you clear instructions — like don't steal — then you gotta trust him. Don't say, "No, God's way won't work in *this* situation." Or when God promises, "Call to me and I will answer you" (Jeremiah 33:3), then trust that he'll *do* that. Don't try to solve an unsolvable mess alone. But yes, *use* your brain. Yes, think. Yes, plan. But most of all, trust God with your whole heart.

Trust in the Lord for stuff you don't understand and simply can't understand. But don't pack your brains away with last year's Christmas decorations. You still need them.

devotion #76
ODD OLD WORDS

They read from the Book of the Law of God, making it clear and giving the meaning so that the people could understand what was being read.

— Nehemiah 8:8

One day a huge crowd of Jews gathered, and a teacher named Ezra brought out the law of Moses, stood up on a platform, and began reading. But soon people began giving Ezra puzzled looks. See, the Hebrew Scriptures were nearly eight hundred years old! Many Jews spoke mostly Aramaic by then and didn't understand old Hebrew words. So Ezra first read the text *very* clearly, then he paused and explained the difficult words.

This still happens today. If you have a four-hundred-year-old King James version of the Bible and you read, "The rent is made worse" (Mark 2:21), you'd think it was talking about a greedy landlord, right? Wrong. It means the rip in the clothing just got bigger. Or if it talks about "earthquakes, in divers places" (Matthew 24:7), it doesn't mean quakes in the sea where divers dive. It means earthquakes in *different* places.

The great thing about translations like the New International Version (NIV) is that they're written in modern English. Still, even with everyday English, you might not understand some words, right? You may hit a word like *circumcision* and not understand what it means. Grab a dictionary or ask someone — in this case your dad — to explain. Don't just wing it.

If you really want to understand the Bible, start with the four gospels in the New Testament. They're interesting and very easy to understand.

devotion #77

CRAFTY, WINDY TALK

*We will no longer be infants ... blown
here and there by every wind of teaching
and by the cunning craftiness of men
in their deceitful scheming.*

— Ephesians 4:14

Infants will swallow just about any tale.
Literally. You see toddlers chewing away on
storybooks all the time. Even young kids don't
really know what the Bible's about. They just
listen to what adults tell them and believe
them. That's great if those telling the stories
are honest, good-hearted people doing
their best to follow Jesus.

But what if someone's got some
weird ideas, and they're cunning and
crafty and can pass them off as truth?

Then you're in trouble. You can get "blown here and there by every wind of teaching." It's like the big bad wolf's at the door, and your house is made of straw instead of solid bricks. You and the house both get blown away by wolfy's bad-breath tornado. You end up rolling around like a tumbleweed.

Don't wanna be blown here and there by wolfy windbags? Read the Bible for yourself so you know what it says. Start by driving slowly through the Gospels. There are lots of cool, important facts in Matthew, Mark, Luke, and John. Then if someone comes along and tries to blow you away with a deceitful, wild tale, you can pipe up and say, "Hey! The Bible doesn't say that!"

Don't be a toddler and just chew on the book. Read your Bible and get some solid truth inside you. Then you won't be blown away when the blowhards blow.

devotion #78
A PUPIL'S PUPILS OPEN

At the end of your life you will groan ...
"I would not obey my teachers or listen
to my instructors. I have come to
the brink of utter ruin."

— Proverbs 5:11 – 14

That *does* happen, you know. Kids who don't pay attention to their studies or don't obey their teachers and don't work in school often end up doing low-paying jobs like pulling the guts out of dead chickens all day long. And if they're still not serious then, they've got real trouble! They end up on the brink of ruin and wish they could go back to school again and do it right this time around.

You don't have to wait till the end of your life for this reap-what-you-sow principle to kick in. If you don't listen to your teachers, you'll fail math, English, and history. Fail enough subjects, and you'll have to take the whole grade over. What a waste of a year! Or refuse to listen to your instructors — whether it's a swimming instructor or a piano teacher — and you just blew your time and your parents' money.

No one's expecting you to be perfect. What *has* been known to work, however, is to listen to your instructors and teachers and make an effort. Sure, you'll mess up sometimes — we all do — but as long as you're trying to learn, you'll get the most out of what the teacher says.

If you don't wanna groan later on the road to ruin, apply yourself now. Take advantage of your opportunities to study and tune in to your teachers.

Devotion #79
INTELLIGENT DISCUSSIONS

Don't have anything to do with
foolish and stupid arguments, because
you know they produce quarrels.
— 2 Timothy 2:23

Back in New Testament days, many Christians in the city of Ephesus were puffed up with useless knowledge and weird theories. They thought they were cutting-edge smart, but the reality was they wasted their time arguing about stupid stuff. Now, you can argue intelligently about important stuff, but these turkeys were arguing about foolishness, so it didn't take long for them to end up in childish quarrels and shouting matches.

You've probably heard arguments like that, right? Two kids yell back and forth at each other:

"You're stupid!"

"Am not!"

"Are too!"

"No, I'm not! *You* are!"

"Uh-uh. *You* are!"

"You stink!"

"*You* do!"

These quarrels happen when people argue about something dumb like who gets to sit where on the couch or which cartoon superhero is the greatest. No one can prove their point, so soon they don't *try* to give intelligent reasons. They just shout insults.

Some things *are* worth arguing about — in a calm, intelligent manner. For example, if someone says that Abraham Lincoln was a famous baseball player, call him on it. If someone says that the math test is a week away but it's happening tomorrow, set her straight. But if they're arguing about whether angels spend their free time hang gliding in the methane storms of Jupiter, forget it! Who knows? Who cares?

A foolish and stupid quarrel is like a lightbulb that doesn't work properly. It produces a lot of heat but not very much light.

devotion #80
PAYING ATTENTION IN SCHOOL

"For in him we live and move and have our being." As some of your own poets have said, "We are his offspring.'"

— Acts 17:28

When Paul was preaching the gospel to the Greeks of Athens, he had to talk about God in a way they could understand and relate to. So in the sentence above, he quoted lines from *two* well-known Greek poets, Epimenides and Aratus. Another time, Paul recited lines from a comedy written by Menander (1 Corinthians 15:33). When Greek kids went to school in those days, they had to study Greek poets and playwrights, and obviously Paul was paying attention.

When you're sitting in English class bored out of your skull learning about

some poets or writers, you may wonder, "Who *cares*?" Or maybe you're in history class and the teacher's making you memorize the year the Revolutionary War began — and you wonder, "Why on *earth* do I need to know this?" Or maybe you listen and memorize facts just long enough to write your test paper — then forget them all afterward.

That kind of "learning" isn't really learning. It's some kind of bizarre mental gymnastics, but it's not how to get the most out of class time. You should study stuff to actually *learn*. Sure, some information is more important than other stuff, but you never know when the "*un*important" facts will come in handy — and not just to answer some trivia question, either.

You may not see the use of some things you study in school right now, but tune in when you're in class. Those facts may be more valuable than you realize.

devotion #81
EXCELLENT THINKING

Whatever is true, whatever is noble, whatever is right, whatever is pure, whatever is lovely, whatever is admirable — if anything is excellent or praiseworthy — think about such things.

— Philippians 4:8

Back in Paul's day, just like today, there was lots of sick stuff in society, and Paul knew that Christians couldn't help but see and hear some of it. Then it would get stuck in their heads and bum them out. That's probably one reason he told them to think about things that were inspiring and encouraging. Then the good thoughts would bump the garbage thoughts out.

Ever had some song play on and on in your head like some radio you can't shut off? That's tiring enough if it's just plain dumb, but what if it's *bad*? There's a lot of garbage in the world today too, and even if you try to avoid the worst stuff by not watching certain TV shows or hanging with certain kids, some junk will still bombard your brain. So what do you do about it?

Deliberately focus on things that are true and good and pure. That doesn't mean you have to sit around thinking about the Bible all day long or humming hymns — though there *are* times when you should do that. But thinking about *admirable* stuff can mean thinking about your football team. Thinking of *excellent* stuff can be remembering how you got serious airtime while out dirt biking. All this is cool, excellent stuff.

Are your thoughts pure and inspiring and uplifting? The choice is yours. Enjoy good, wholesome fun and fill your mind with pure, excellent thoughts.

Devotion #82
COMMONSENSE SOLUTIONS

My men will haul them down from Lebanon to the sea, and I will float them in rafts by sea to the place you specify.

— 1 Kings 5:9

King Solomon needed thousands of tons of cedarwood to build the temple of God. Cedar trees grew in King Hiram's land in the mountains of Lebanon. So Hiram said he'd have his men chop down the trees, drag them to the sea, and float them to some port in Israel. You notice Hiram didn't try to drag those monster logs a hundred miles overland from Tyre to Jerusalem. It was far easier to float those supersized suckers down the coast!

Sometimes what seem like totally huge problems and obstacles have

simple solutions. Say you need to do your homework, but none of your pencils has a point and your pencil sharpener has vanished into the crack of doom along with Frodo's ring. Since you can't do your homework, you might as well goof off, right? Or what if you can't find your swimming trunks? Do you miss out on a swim?

Don't give up easily. Think *simple solutions*. Your official sharpener might have evaporated, but there are other ways to get your pencil up and running. Like, you could ask your dad to sharpen it with a kitchen knife. (Don't try this yourself.) It's primitive, but it works. Lost your trunks? Wear your gym shorts. Again, primitive, but so what?

Work smarter, not harder. Solutions don't need to be things of beauty to work. They just need to work.

devotion #83
GOD GUIDING YOUR MIND

Then David gave his son
Solomon ... the plans of all that
the Spirit had put in his mind for
the courts of the temple.

— 1 Chronicles 28:11 – 12

When David found out that God wanted his son Solomon to build a temple, David drew up the designs for the building. Then all Solomon had to do was follow directions. David probably had zero experience in designing temples, so where'd he get his ideas? God's Spirit gave him the plans. Sure, David knew what Phoenician temples looked like — and Bible scholars say he borrowed ideas from them — but for the most part he did the design with God's help.

God gave you a mind — and he's hoping you'll use it — but he doesn't leave you on your own. God's like a *tutor*, a special one-on-one teacher. When you have a tutor, you still have to think hard and work to figure things out, but the tutor's looking over your shoulder, explaining and helping each step of the way. God was like that with David. God kept David's thoughts moving in the right direction.

If you're a Christian and have God in your life, then his Spirit can guide you each step of the way. He will give you cool counsel and teach you. John 14:26 says, "The Counselor, the Holy Spirit . . . will teach you all things and will remind you of everything I have said to you."

Want to succeed? Think things through and plan well, but also pray for spiritual downloads. Ask God to put his plans in your mind.

Devotion #84
PARENTS' BRAINPOWER

Listen, my son, to your father's instruction and do not forsake your mother's teaching. They will be ... a chain to adorn your neck.

— Proverbs 1:8 – 9

Proverbs is full of wise sayings. This wise saying sounds a lot like the fifth commandment, which says, "Honor your father and your mother" (Exodus 20:12). God wants you to respect your parents ... even if you don't think they're so smart. Just do it. Going into a little more detail than the commandment, this Proverb tells you to listen to your dad because he's lived life, knows a thing or two, and is worth listening to.

The Proverb goes on to tell you not to "forsake your mother's teaching." When you were young, Mom was probably the one who taught you stuff, reminded you of rules, and talked to you when you messed up. Now that you're older and not a small kid anymore, you might think you don't need to listen to Mom any longer. Maybe you wanna impress your friends by sassing her or ignoring her.

Do yourself a favor — don't do it. Your mom and dad knew what they were talking about all those years, so don't ditch their teachings now. It's all still good. Stuff like being responsible and tidy, having manners, etc., is still important. Besides the fact that your parents are smart, they're looking out for you. They want what's best for you.

Ever see some superathlete with a glittering gold chain around his neck? That's how your spirit will be decked out if you listen to your parents.

Devotion #85
ZONED OUT AND DISTRACTED

While your servant was busy here and there, the man disappeared.

—1 Kings 20:40

One time a prophet dressed up like a soldier to tell King Ahab a story. He basically said, "I was in the thick of battle when someone brought me this superimportant prisoner and said, 'Drop everything and guard this prisoner! Don't let him escape! If he goes missing, you're dead!'" Well, in this story, sure enough, the soldier got busy with this and that, he took his eyes off the prisoner, and the man slipped away.

What about you? How easily do you zone out and get sidetracked? Your mom tells you to clean your room before dinner, but as you're picking up your books you get sucked into

reading a comic. Or you're taking your dirty clothes to the laundry, but on your way you see your broken skateboard so you get busy fixing it. Next thing you know, it's dinnertime, your laundry's heaped in the hall, and your room's still a disaster.

If you allow yourself to get distracted, there'll be consequences. You really wanna avoid consequences if you can — and you *can*! If you know that you're easily distracted, determine to get a grip on this problem and overcome it. That's half the battle right there. When you're given a responsibility or told to do something, stay focused. Discipline yourself. Remind yourself that there will be consequences if you don't.

The zone-out stuff may be interesting. But it you want to avoid trouble, don't allow it to derail you from what you're supposed to do.

devotion #86
TRIVIA AND JUNK INFORMATION

All the Athenians and the foreigners who lived there spent their time doing nothing but talking about and listening to the latest ideas.

— Acts 17:21

The guys in Athens, Greece, really wanted to be on top of stuff! Anything new that blew into town, they had to check it out. These guys liked to just sit around all day blabbing about new ideas — not necessarily important stuff, either. They were into trivia. They were junk-information junkies. They sure liked to talk and show off what they knew.

Now, if you're into baseball and love memorizing lists of batting averages, go for it! If you love *Star Trek* and want

to be a trekkie, trek on! (Just don't set your brain
to *stunned*.) But if that's all you do — like, if you do
nothing but that — you are tripped off, dude! You can
get into trivia so much that you miss living life itself.

Don't forget to comb your hair, do your
homework, and live a life beyond TV and baseball
cards. Get outside and breathe some fresh air! Go
out and actually play baseball. Your hobby will still be
waiting for you. The joystick will still be hooked up to
the game box. But in the meantime, break out of your
zombie state and live!

It's okay to be fascinated by trivia and keen to
learn new stats and facts, but whatever you're into, you
gotta take breaks from it and come up for air.

Devotion #87
BUCKLE DOWN AND DO IT

*Those who are wayward in spirit
will gain understanding; those who
complain will accept instruction.*

— Isaiah 29:24

When someone is *wayward* it means
they've wandered off the way and gone astray.
Think of a field trip. Your class hikes to a
fish farm, but you leave the path to chase
a skunk through the woods. You are
wayward, dude! You won't pass *Go*,
you won't collect $200, and you won't
learn anything about fish. (True, you'll
learn a lot about how skunks defend
themselves.) Wayward can also be a
lazy kid doing whatever he can to get
out of homework.

It's great that "those who complain will [finally!] accept instruction," but right now these dudes are groaning and complaining and *not* accepting instruction. The reason they're complaining (besides the fact that it's a habit) is they have the idea that if they complain enough, they'll get out of cleaning their room or doing their homework or brushing their teeth. That's not how things work in the real world.

A big part of growing up is when you realize that, like it or not, there are things you *have* to do — so you do them without mumbling every step of the way. And since most wayward, wandering, murmuring complainers eventually *do* buckle down and do what they're supposed to (because they can't get out of it), they might as well smarten up and stop complaining now.

When you stop chasing skunks through the woods, buckle down and get busy learning — that's when you gain understanding.

devotion #88
THE OTHER SIDE OF THE STORY

The first to present his case seems
right, till another comes forward
and questions him.

— Proverbs 18:17

In ancient Israel, just like today, when people
had disputes they dragged the matter to court.
Since each guy was convinced he was right,
he passionately argued that such-and-such
belonged to him, or that some accident was
the other guy's fault. Guy Number One could
be pretty convincing. But when it was Guy
Number Two's turn to talk, he'd bring up all
the details that Guy One had deliberately
left out.

Ever get in a fight with your
brother and then go running to your

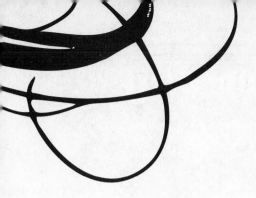

mom saying, "He hit me!"? So your mom calls your brother into the kitchen and she's ready to send him to his room or the dungeons. But when your brother limps into the kitchen he asks, "Did you tell Mom you kicked me first?" (Oh, yeah . . . *that* little detail.)

If you're fastest up the stairs to tell your tale of woe first, you'll seem right, but even if your brother crawls slowly up the stairs, he will eventually get there and tell his side of the story. Remember the cartoon movie *Hoodwinked*? Everybody was blaming everybody else for what had happened, but it turned out they were all mistaken. It was the evil little bunny all along.

There's usually more than one side to a story. Listen to all sides before you make up your mind. And if you're telling your side, make sure to tell not only the truth but the *whole* truth.

Devotion #89
FALSE KNOWLEDGE

Turn away from godless
chatter and the opposing ideas of
what is falsely called knowledge.

— 1 Timothy 6:20

Greeks in New Testament times were big into education and learning, which was great! Some Greeks were really deep thinkers, and that's cool. Pythagoras, for example, is said to have discovered the Pythagorean theorem — a complicated math formula. He also decided that the world was round two thousand years before Columbus thought of it. But some Greeks took this deep-thinking stuff too far. They dreamed up complicated theories about God and creation and called their guesses "secret knowledge."

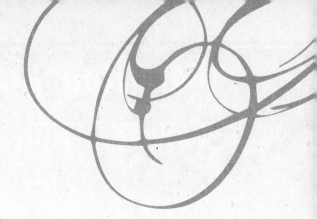

There are lots of theories and guesswork *falsely* called knowledge today too. People earn a lot of money writing wild books about the Bible and what it "really" means and what "really" happened. They write complex theories about how Jesus was never crucified, how he never died, etc. The Gospels tell it like it was, yet some people try to explain it all sideways and say that it means something totally different.

In recent years, many people have invented "opposing ideas" to avoid believing the simple, straightforward message of the Bible. The apostle Paul said that such ideas were about as intelligent as "godless chatter," and he said to turn away from them. By the way, if you wanna know what chatter is, picture a budgie bird on steroids that chirps and chatters all day long and simply will *not* shut up.

If you want real knowledge, read the Bible and accept it at face value. Turn away from the chattering false knowledge men invent to oppose God's Word.

Devotion #90
REASONABLE FAITH

*"I am not insane, most excellent Festus,"
Paul replied. "What I am saying is
true and reasonable."*

— Acts 26:25

When the apostle Paul was explaining his faith to the Roman governor Festus, things were going fine until Paul talked about Jesus coming back to life from the dead. Festus nearly jumped out of his throne. "You are out of your mind, Paul!" he shouted. "Your great learning is driving you insane!" Paul denied being bonkers and insisted that what he was saying was true. It really happened. Not only that, but Christianity is reasonable — it all makes sense.

Some skeptics joke that you have to leave your brains at the door to believe in God. "You gotta take the Bible by faith," they say, "because it makes no sense." Oh, man! Way, waaaay out to lunch! That is simply not so. Christianity is the most reasonable faith of all. The Bible isn't a bunch of fluffy poetry and myths like most religions. Bible characters were real people who lived on earth in real time.

Archaeologists are scientists who dig in the earth to learn about ancient people and civilizations. One thing they've discovered time and time again is that the Bible is right! They've dug up tons of tablets and evidence in Israel and other places that prove the events the Bible described really happened and its facts are true and reasonable.

Don't leave your brains at the door when reading the Bible. You'll need them to examine the solid facts your faith is built upon.

Devotions to Make You Stronger

Written by Ed Strauss

Softcover • ISBN 0-310-71311-0

NIV 2:52 Backpack Bible

Italian Duo-Tone™, Brown/Orange

ISBN 0-310-71417-6

The full NIV text in a handy size
for boys on the go—
for ages 8 and up.

Available now at your local bookstore!

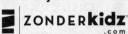